Dear Lizzie

Dear Lizzie

Memoir of a Jewish Immigrant Woman

Leona Tamarkin

Edited with an Introduction by Elizabeth Reis

Library of Congress Number:		00-192232
ISBN #:	Hardcover	0-7388-3912-4
	Softcover	0-7388-3913-2

This book was printed in the United States of America.

To order additional copies of this book, contact:
Xlibris Corporation
1-888-7-XLIBRIS
www.Xlibris.com
Orders@Xlibris.com

Contents

TO THE MEMORY OF MY DEAR HUSBAND,
JOSEPH B. TAMARKIN

Acknowledgments

Many family members deserve thanks for urging me to "do something with Grandma's story." My parents, Pamela Tamarkin Reis (Leona Tamarkin's older daughter) and Ronald Reis were very supportive throughout, eager to see it appear in print, but also understanding when other projects had to take precedence for a time. Allan, Maurry, and Stanley Tamarkin, and Sasha Tamarkin Sedan, Leona Tamarkin's other children, also waited patiently and offered their encouragement.

I would like to thank several friends who read either the manuscript, the introduction, or both. My Jewish Feminist Reading Group read the memoir and inspired me just as I was about to begin writing the introduction. Thanks to Judith Raiskin, Mary Wood, Ajuan Nance, Clare Kinberg, Diane Baxter, Ellen Rifkin, Maram Epstein, Irene Diamond, and Arlene Stein. Thank you also to Naomi Kirtner, Ray Birn, Cynthia Eller, and Pamela Tamarkin Reis for their fine editorial suggestions, to Julie Tamarkin for typing much of Leona's original story, and to Suzanne Whiteley, Maxine Seller and Rudolph Vecoli for their assistance. My husband and fellow historian, Matthew Dennis, tirelessly read and edited endless drafts despite his own demanding schedule; his criticism was as constructive as it was perceptive. I am indebted, as always.

Finally, I am grateful to Leona Tamarkin for opening up her heart and her past to me and for others to share. That my children, Sam and Leah Reis-Dennis, have gotten to know their great-grandmother is a wonderful blessing.

Introduction

For many years I have assigned my grandmother's story, *Dear Lizzie*, to my undergraduate classes in United States Women's History at the University of Oregon. Few students know before they read it that Leona Tamarkin is my grandmother, and most are surprised when I tell them that this is my family's story. Students cannot believe that, despite overwhelming adversity, the girl in the narrative grew up, had five children, that those children had children, and that I, one of those grandchildren, am standing in front of them, a living embodiment of family—and Jewish—preservation.

My grandmother's story moved them to tears, but more important for students of history, it gave immediacy and humanity to distant historical events. The European events of the First World War seem as ancient as the Peloponnesian War to my students, so far removed are they from this tragedy. *Dear Lizzie* draws them in and enables them to enter this distant world. Through Leona Tamarkin's memory, readers glimpse Europe's devastation during the First World War and gain an understanding of what it meant to emigrate to the United States in those postwar years. Leona's story sounds like many of my students' own family immigrant stories (no matter where they are from). She is self-educated, as so many immigrants of that period were, and the narrative's simplicity and naivete reveals the universality of a certain kind of childhood experience that was and is shared by many immigrants. Her writing has an easy spontaneity about it that suggests nature rather than artifice, the recounting of memory rather than the crafting of a story.

Leona Tamarkin was fifteen years old when she came with her older sister to America. Her memoir begins when she was just a small girl in Brest-Litovsk, in Russian-occupied Poland. Born in 1905, Tamarkin relates her experiences as a Jewish refugee, as the German and, later, the Russian armies entered village after village, forcing inhabitants to flee their brief havens and seek sanctuary elsewhere. Tamarkin's story chronicles the hardships her family endured: her parents' divorce on the eve of her father's emigration to America before the war (decreed by the rabbi just in case her father failed to reunite the family in the New World), her mother's early death, her own and her older sister's and brother's near starvation as refugees. The reader rejoices when, finally, her father finds their names on a Jewish social service agency's list and sends them money and tickets to America.

Tamarkin's memoir highlights one important truth about twentieth-century Jewish history in Europe: that it was not confined to Europe. The dislocation of European Jewry during the First World War and its later devastation in the Holocaust is fundamentally part of American Jewish history as well. In reading this powerful story, we are reminded that "immigration" cannot be appreciated without an understanding of European events. To challenge the adage on the nature of history, the past is *not* a foreign country; indeed, as William Faulkner wrote, "It's not even past."

As a child, Tamarkin was aware of the seismic changes she faced, and her writing transports readers back to those frightening ordeals. What makes her story exceptional is that she recollects the child's point of view so vividly. The child's perspective and voice guides the narrative, carrying readers not only to the historical time and place, but to that time in our own lives when we were small children. After Leona's father divorces her mother and leaves for America, the small girl is embarrassed when her classmates tease her about not having a father. Similarly, the agony she feels when made to wear a dress her mother fashions out of a red silk man's shirt parallels comparable self-conscious moments we all have faced. Tamarkin's writing style allows readers to empathize with the protagonists. It is not that we feel sorrow for the author as a grown-up woman; we feel sorry for that little girl, suffering pain and living daily with fear and hunger.

As modern readers, and as Americans who, thankfully, have not experienced war in our own country, our hearts go out to this girl, not only because of the gnawing hunger, which most of us have never endured, but because we can identify with her as a child, which we have all been; we can share her confusion about her world and how to act in it properly, and her fears of the uncertain consequences she faces from parents and others, for her misdeeds. She conveys her sense that the rules for acceptable conduct have been altered during wartime, and she struggles to negotiate the new terrain. Previously punishable acts are now ignored; seemingly innocuous activity now brings down wrath, inexplicably to a child's mind. In the tumult she tries to determine how she might maintain some sense of the rules that govern her unsettled world.

The memoir depicts the horrendous social chaos that accompanies war. Leona recounts the shocked incredulity of Brest-Litovsk's residents when instructed simply to vacate their homes in 1915. Anticipating that the enemy would make use of the nearby ammunitions dump, government officials told all citizens to leave—to where, nobody knew. The turmoil, the packing, the heartbreak of leaving one's home and life, the uncertainty of refugee status, being blindly marched about or shuttled by railcars: all is succinctly and lucidly reported. As a piece of Jewish history, this narrative helps us to understand how individuals reconciled their Jewish identity with the hard facts of anti-Semitism. Pre-war anti-Semitic legislation forced many Jewish workers, including Leona's father, to leave the country to look for work. As refugees, the Jews of Poland found themselves without a home.

Leona's story belongs to women's history as well as to Jewish or immigration history. The genre of women's autobiography is growing, and these accounts occupy a literary niche as well as a historical one. Jewish women's autobiographies like Rose Cohen's *Out of the Shadow,* Rose Pesotta's *Bread Upon the Waters,* or Emma Goldman's *Living My Life* feature the lives of autonomous and rebellious women, and introduce us to a relatively neglected aspect of Jewish culture: the charismatic activities of Jewish immigrant women in public life. Tamarkin offers a somewhat different perspective. She is not remembered for her labor or political activism. She never became famous. Her story exemplifies the experiences of the majority of women immigrants, remembered only among their families and friends, whose lives are nonetheless important as historical testimony.

Writing one's autobiography, in and of itself, is an unconventional act. Traditionally, women have written their lives far less frequently than have men. Leona wrote not for fame, but so that her story would not be forgotten. When, as a fifteen year old girl, I asked my grandmother to tell me about the time when she was my age, she started to speak but began to cry instead. On several occasions she wanted to tell me, but the pain was still close to her heart, even after over sixty years. My mother suggested she write it down for me, and this writing became an important part of my grandmother's life. She showed it to someone at the community college she attended in New Haven, Connecticut, and he passed it along to a man who had received a grant to build ties between the community's elderly and youth. Her story was scripted and performed in area high schools for several years. My grandmother played the lead—she would have it no other way—while another senior played her mother and her sister, and an elderly man played her father and brother.

Leona's fiery personality is unmistakable in this account. Her determination, will to live, and boldness, even within confining circumstances, singles her out. Again and again in her memoir, we can catch glimpses of what sets this girl apart from her peers. Tamarkin describes daring escapades before the war, rolling logs as loggers do, or hiking several hours away from the security of her home. Assertions of her individuality ripple through this memoir.

Insights about the gendered nature of Tamarkin's world flow easily from the narrative. Leona is thoughtful about her experience as a girl growing up, and she is sensitive to the inequitable gender differences she encountered. Reading her account, we can begin to learn what it was like to be a young girl in turn-of-the-century Poland. After she reaches the United States, she provides a gendered picture of immigrant life. Like many girls, Leona wanted to be a boy at various times during her childhood. She isn't allowed to play *polante* (baseball) like her brother; she would sometimes get to hit the ball, but she is not permitted to run the bases because that privilege is reserved for the boys.

In this memoir, girls and women still perform "women's work" despite their living conditions. Laundry, for example, falls to the women. Leona's sister, Mollie, desperately looking for some way to avoid starvation, takes in the soldiers' white shirts in order to earn a few pennies, while her brother awakens at 4:30 A.M. each morning and walks seven miles to his work on a farm. Laundry is what Mollie knows how to do and what society considers a woman's job. The soldiers, poor enough themselves, will nevertheless pay to be rid of this unmanly task.

Leona's story implicitly raises the question of feminism. Though the author experienced the feminist movement of the 1960s and 70s, she never joins the movement nor identifies herself as a feminist because it never occurs to her that she is not the equal of any man. She has faced and surmounted inequities of opportunity and believes in equality of the sexes as she believes in breathing. Her life has been imbued with the spirit, if not the label, of feminism.

During the First World War, when Leona is struggling to survive her childhood, gender rules are at once fundamentally overturned and superficially retained; women do whatever they need to do, and they do it with the skills at their disposal. With fathers, husbands, and brothers no longer able to provide protection and support, women tailor (often literally) their skills to the marketplace. What we now think of as feminist traits—independence, determination, courage, and fortitude—were to Leona and her sister Mollie the unisex tools of survival.

Tamarkin's perspective on womanhood has been shaped by her experience as a wartime survivor. And much of this frame of reference looks rather "traditional." For Leona, women should be strong and nurturing, the builders and conservators of family. In quest of stability and "normality," she acts assertively, both confirming and challenging conventional roles of women's, and girls', place. The extraordinary account of this ordinary woman challenges us to search for the complexities in the lives of common women working through, with, and against apparently confining traditions and gender prescriptions.

Leona wants desperately to come to America, and she sees it from the very beginning as the Golden Land. Everything Leona encounters is a wonder; even the food she eats on the journey is far more abundant than she had imagined in her wildest dreams. Her fears center, not on what life will bring when she arrives, but rather on what would become of her if she were sent back by immigration officials for a failed medical examination.

Tamarkin's memoir is richly revealing of immigrant life in both St. Louis and New York City. She describes her various jobs as a seamstress in the garment industry and her phenomenal success as a piece worker. Week after week she wins the bonus money offered by her employer, and she has fun spending the money with her girlfriends. As she relives the romance with her future husband, Joe, we can feel her happiness and good fortune. Descriptions of the "Saturday Street" in St. Louis show the delight with which their family embraces American life, and the depiction of gatherings at the Pavilion in Forest Park evokes the essence of a vital Jewish immigrant community. During the Depression of the 1930s, Leona and Joe struggled as Joe resourcefully devised money-making ventures and Leona endured difficult pregnancies. Together, with the financial help of extended family in St. Louis they managed to eke out a living and create a life together.

For Leona, now far removed—at least physically—from wartime hardships, learning to live in a free country would have its own difficulties. Survivors cannot simply banish the past from their minds. Leona recalls, for example, her momentary fright when she mistakes a backfiring car engine for gunfire. And she is amazed that people in America could live their lives so nonchalantly, without fear. Americans' complacency even angers her. Full of rage, she thinks, "how can people go so quietly about their lives when other human beings are being torn to pieces?"

The title of this book, *Dear Lizzie*, reminds us that the story was first conveyed as a letter from a grandmother to her granddaughter. The memories needed to be written down privately because the words were too painful to say out loud. It reminds us that, though physical suffering has been alleviated, emotional wounds may still exist. Survivors learn, if they are lucky, how to cope in the world, but just below the surface are the loss and the memories, at times unutterable. Even Leona, who seemingly had moved beyond these sad years, cried as she began to relate her life story to me when I was fifteen. Her account emphasizes, I believe, that the larger story of immigration to America is more complex than the "happily ever after" fairy tale ending. Still, Leona's narrative exudes confidence, excitement, and appreciation of life's possibilities notwithstanding its sorrows and disappointments. As an immigrant, Leona Tamarkin is more grateful than doubtful. I can hear her impatiently saying now, "Of course I was happy to be here! Why wouldn't I be happy?"

Chapter One

My fifteen year old granddaughter asked me to tell her about my childhood, what life was like sixty-nine years ago in Brest-Litovsk, Poland.

My dear Lizzie,

There was no television, no radio, no funnies in the newspapers, nor did we have the dozens of toys most children now have. Life wasn't dull as you may think. We didn't miss the things that didn't yet exist.

In the summer we played hop-scotch; the boys played a game called *polante* which was baseball. It surprised me very much when I came to the States and found grown men playing the same game. This game was a great sorrow to me, for I wasn't allowed to play it. My brother, Moshe, would stand up for me, and since it was his ball, I sometimes got a turn at bat. But I wasn't allowed to run the bases. Most products that now come packed in boxes came in barrels. One could always find a discarded iron rim from a barrel. You rolled it along with a stick. You won if you rolled the rim longest without it falling down.

We had wooden sidewalks, but the street was not paved. A lot of time was spent building castles in the sand which was white and clean. In the summer after a rain, we were allowed to go barefoot. For some reason that gave us a lot of pleasure. We also played "Ring Around the Rosie," though the song was different.

Winters were hard. When snow came in early fall it stayed

the whole winter. Snow would pile on snow; none of it would melt until late May. My sister, Mollie, would make rag dolls for me, and she would even play dress-up with me though she was seven years older than I. It was my nagging that made her stoop so low.

The best thing I liked was when we had visitors. I was a talkative child, but only in secret. When I was alone I would tell myself stories; when adults were around I was very quiet. No one knew I was there listening. There were two girls, sisters, who would come every Saturday morning. The older one must have been in her twenties; she had black fuzzy hair and her skin was muddy. The younger one was about eighteen; she had reddish brown hair, rosy cheeks, and brown flashing eyes. They talked about marriage. They were angry at their parents for not finding husbands for them as yet. I always looked forward to Saturday morning; it was such a jolly time. But I think my mother got tired of their talk, for she told my sister that is the last time they will come. I missed them very much for there wasn't anything to do on a Saturday. I really couldn't understand my mother.

I remember there were other times my mother and I disagreed, but my disagreement was in silence. I would sit on my little chair in the kitchen and watch my mother make my rice and milk or noodles and milk. (I couldn't stand to eat meat. Of course at first my mother tried to make me eat what she cooked for the others, but I would gag, and she had to give up.) Sitting on my chair, with my little table in front of me, I would compose long, and to my mind very just, arguments that I planned to make to my mother when the proper time came to prove I was right and she was in the wrong. The proper time never came.

We had a round dining room table that had a center post. The post separated into four legs. The sections between the legs were separate countries to me. I would sit under the table and tell myself stories of the distant lands I heard grownups talk about. I moved from section to section, and in each part I was a rich merchant from England, France, Germany, and Italy. These were the only distant countries I had heard about. I wanted to travel and see everything.

When I was a little older I stopped playing under the table and went out to explore the world. My intention was to walk as far as I could on the street we lived on and then walk back. I couldn't get lost. I came to a very wide street. An island of grass and trees separated one side of the street from the other. I felt it was too wide a street for me to cross; still, it was too short a walk. I didn't see too much of the world. The street I was walking on wasn't too wide; I could cross it and walk along my side of the wide street. There was a sign I couldn't miss—a big white house with a white fence around it. There were street signs, but I couldn't read them.

I crossed the street and walked on. After a while, becoming tired, I turned back and looked for the white house with the fence. I found one and walked on that street. The sun was going down and my feet hurt, but no sign of my house. I realized I picked the wrong white house. I was terribly frightened. I started running and crying like a wild animal. People did stop me and ask what was the trouble, but they couldn't help me. I didn't know the name of the street I lived on. I found the right white house and came home after dark. Although I knew my mother never spanked me, for this I thought she will spank me—as hard as she spanked my brother and sister. When she spanked them and they cried, my skin would shiver. Now I will really get it. But I had to go into the house; where else could I go. I walked into the kitchen. My mother said, "Sit down. Your rice is almost ready." Nowadays it may seem odd that my mother wasn't worried not seeing me the whole afternoon, but there wasn't anything to worry about. Children weren't kidnapped in those days; everyone had plenty of their own.

When I was four or five tragedy struck our family. One morning as my mother was getting my two brothers ready for *cheder* (school), the younger one complained of a headache. My mother felt his head; it was hot. She put him to bed. His fever kept on rising. There were no telephones in the city except those used in business houses. My mother sent my sister to a relative for him to get the doctor. Why my sister wasn't sent directly for the doctor, I don't know. Perhaps she didn't know where he lived.

The doctor didn't come the same day. When he came, he told my mother she had a very sick boy. He called it "inflammation of the brain." That was a name given to a patient's illness when the doctor couldn't diagnose the case. He prescribed something, took his money, and went on his way. A few days later my brother got worse. The doctor was called again. He came, prescribed something else, and went on his way. My brother's breathing became very heavy; his face became flushed. To this day I can hear my poor brother beg, "Mother, help me. Please help me." She would sit on his bed, cry, and wring her hands. What else could she do? One early dawn I was awakened by loud cries. My brother had just died. He was eight years old. He had blue eyes and blond curly hair. His name was Isaac. My mother never got over the loss of her beautiful son. My dear Lizzie, I must stop for a while. My eyes are blinded with tears.

I was born in 1905, the child of a second marriage for both my parents. My mother's first husband died when he was only twenty-six. He left her with three small children, a girl, Mollie, and two boys, Moshe and Isaac. My father's first wife died in childbirth with her second son. When my parents got married, there was already a family of five children. It didn't work out. When I was about a year old, my parents separated. It was my mother's wish. She said her step-sons were driving her to an early grave.

It was to be a separation for a while only until my father's sons grew a little older and went to school and were more manageable. My father waited for that reunion for eleven years. It never came about; by that time my mother was dead. My father could have married someone else years before that because my parents were finally divorced, but my father waited on. The divorce was forced on him, and he meant to remarry my mother.

I will tell you about that later. Now I will tell you about my father kidnapping me when I was about two years old.

My father wanted me to live with him. My mother said I was too young to leave her care. One day my father passed our house. I was playing in the front yard. He picked me up and took me home with him. I don't remember that part; I do remember an old woman (that was my grandmother) giving me food, and I remember crying a lot.

When I was missing, my mother knew who took me. She made no move to get me back. My sister and brothers wanted her to get me back, but she said that my father had as much right to me as she did. Besides, my grandmother would soon tire of taking care of two rambunctious boys and a little girl. She was right, but I was gone long enough to forget her. My brothers and sister used to go to my father's house every day, stand in front of the window, and try to get a glimpse of me. I was usually there, and they would wave at me and I would wave back. I remember that too, but I didn't know who they were.

My father had to take me back to my mother. He was ashamed to have to give in. He brought me back at night, put me on the porch, knocked on the door, and quickly walked away. I started to cry. My mother came out, picked me up and made me nice, but I started to cry even louder. I didn't know her. A Polish woman came out to see what the commotion was all about. I remember she took me from my mother's arms and spoke soothingly to me. I finally subsided into small sobs. That is all I remember of that night. Nor do I remember anything in between then and the next time I saw my father. But that is another tale.

Soon after this incident my father moved to Warsaw. I must have been about four when one day I was called in from play to be washed and scrubbed. A new dress was put on me; the one my father sent from Warsaw I was told. My father was coming to visit me. I didn't know what "father" meant.

There were mysterious whisperings between my mother and sister. My mother was saying she won't let it happen again. When

I was much older my sister told me that she was afraid my father was coming to take me away. Soon a strange man came into the house. The other children were sent out to play; only I was to remain. A terrible fear struck me; something bad was going to happen to me. The man tried to pick me up. I kicked and struggled with all my might. My mother said, "Leave her alone, Yitzhak. She will soon get used to you." He took out a gold piece and told me if I will sit on his lap, he will give it to me. He won me over. I didn't know its value, but it looked beautiful.

Then the real talk started. The man said, "Well, Pessie, it is time for us to get together and be one family again." I don't remember my mother's exact words, but it seemed my father was away from home too much. She didn't think she could manage her two step-sons. I was busy playing with my gold piece and my father's watch. It started getting dark; my brothers and sister were called in. Lamps were lighted. We ate, and my father finally left. They had come to no agreement, for things remained as they were.

The next time I saw my father, I remembered him. I asked for a gold piece. He came with his two sons, Jacob and Albert. They had come to say good-bye; they were going to America. My father had lost the means of making a living. My father was a railroad contractor. That is what it was called. He didn't build railroads; he had charge of a certain amount of railroad track. He had a crew of men that did repairing on his amount of mileage. After that there was another contractor and so on and so on. He traveled with the crew on the train and was only home on weekends.

An *ukase* (a proclamation or order by a Russian emperor or government, having the force of law) had come that the Jews were no longer to be given such contracts. My father decided to go to a free country where his livelihood could not be taken away from him because he was a Jew. My parents came to an agreement that as soon as my father got established in the new country he would send for my mother and the children. That is, her children and me; his sons, Jacob and Albert, were going with him.

Jolly good-byes were said all around. There was just one little thing that marred the happy occasion. Jacob, my father's older son, picked me up and said, "Let's take her with us now." I kicked and scratched his face. He dropped me. I fell into a puddle and splashed mud on his new suit.

I don't know how it started; perhaps my mother told a neighbor and that one told another. It got to the chief Rabbi of Brest-Litovsk that my father was going to America. There were cases where men left wives and children in the old country, went to America, and were never heard from again. Nothing could be done in a case like that; no one knew beforehand if a man would send for his wife. My mother's case was different. She and her husband had not lived under the same roof for several years. Therefore there was less chance of his sending for her. The Rabbi sent for my mother and told her she will have to get a divorce, for if she never hears from her estranged husband, she will never be able to marry again. The Rabbi said it wasn't right for a Jewish young woman to spend the rest of her life alone.

The Rabbi was a famous man; he must have been a good talker. Besides, the Rabbi laid down the law and you did as you were told. My mother agreed to the divorce though she kept on saying she will not marry again. The Rabbi wrote to the chief Rabbi in Warsaw and explained to him the situation. He got in touch with my father, but there was a tougher nut to crack. My father positively refused to divorce my mother.

I don't know what pressure was used. My father finally gave in, and my mother was sent for. The divorce papers came by mail. I believe that papers were put in my mother's hands in front of witnesses, and she was divorced. The government had nothing to do with matters like that. The rabbis married and the rabbis divorced.

All this I heard my mother discuss with neighbors and relatives. I was entirely unconcerned about the matter. When I grew older and my little friends would talk about their fathers, I realized it would be nice to have a father. As far as I understood, my mother didn't have a husband; therefore, I didn't have a father. Sometimes my friends would ask me where my father was; they never see him. I was so deeply ashamed that I didn't have a father that I would lie to them and tell them that my father never left the house. I was very much teased about it. They would say that surely on Friday night he has to go to *shul*, and they saw my mother going to *shul* alone. It could have been easily explained to me that I do have a father, and that someday we will all go to him; the divorce was only to last until my father sent for us and then my parents would remarry. They now talk of generation gaps. The generation gap that then existed between parent and child was insurmountable. I would as soon ask questions of my mother as fly to the moon. Now they even do that. I suffered my shame in silence.

America was a land of riches. No one gave much thought how they were going to go about making their fortunes. God will help. My father thought that in one year or two he would be able to send for us. He had no profession, no manual skills. He didn't know the language. He soon saw his few rubles melting away. The closest he'd come to manual labor was watching his crew of men using a hammer and nails. He got a job as a carpenter in New York. He was soon fired.

My father had relatives in St. Louis—an older sister and a younger brother. He wrote them, told them how bad things were with him, and they sent him money to come to St. Louis. He got a job as a carpenter with the Freund Baking Company. In those days bread was delivered to the grocers in the small hours of the morning. A wooden box was put near the door of the store. The delivery man put the bread in the box and locked it. He and the grocer had the only keys to the box. In time my father became a fine cabinet maker. He worked for that company for over thirty years until he retired.

Chapter Two

About a mile from the edge of a town ran the river Bug. Sometimes on hot days my mother would organize a swimming party with a neighbor woman or two and their daughters. It had to be all females because we swam in the nude. I would hardly call it a swimming party, for no one knew how to swim. We would splash around in the water and were never allowed to go any farther than a few feet from the little bit of sandy shore. Farther down the river was the men's place where my brother and other boys would splash around. Both sides of the river were overgrown with rushes and trees. It was a lonely wilderness. There was little traffic on the river. Very seldom we would see a small boat and then crouch down until it had passed.

The river was really a logging highway. When spring came thousands of timbers would come down to a lumber mill where men with long poles with hooks on them would pull them to shore. The manager of the works had a little girl my age. The family lived on the grounds. Here is where I spent most of my summer days.

The whole yard was enclosed by a fence. There was one wide gate through which one could enter. There was always a watchman there, and no other children but myself were allowed to come in. Then I thought I was someone special; now I know that place was too dangerous for children to play in. The little girl needed someone to play with. Our mothers were friends so I was elected. I liked going there to play because there was a lot of room to run around. There were railroad tracks at one end near the river that were fun to walk on. There were stacks of boards put out to dry that we climbed. Then there was the river. In the spring when the logs started coming down, we spent whole days watching the loggers. It seemed so easy to stand on the logs when the logs rolled. The men just moved their feet a little and were always on top.

Once we came to the river, and there was no one about. I told my friend we should climb on a log and sail it like the loggers do. She didn't want to do it, but she said she would watch me. One end of a log was caught on the shore, and so I climbed on it. As I got on, it drifted away a little, and then it gave a roll. I couldn't keep my footing as the loggers do. I laid down on the log, and I held on tight. The log gave another roll; my head and shoulders were in the water, my legs up in the air. I kicked and struggled to right myself. I was drowning. With my last bit of strength I got my head out of the water. Somehow I got to the shore where my friend was standing and laughing. I asked Cipha why she didn't run for help when she saw me drowning. She said I looked so funny with my head in the water and my legs kicking up in the air, she didn't want to leave the sight.

All my clothes were wet. I was afraid to go home; my mother told me never to go near the river. Besides, the punishment I would get would mean that I could never go there again. Shivering from cold and crying from fear, I went to Cipha's mother and sobbed out my troubles. She took off my clothes, hung them out to dry, and put me to bed with a hot water bottle. By the time my clothes got dry, it was getting dark. To iron my clothes would involve making hot coals, putting them in the iron, and waiting until it got hot. Cipha's mother put my clothes on me and sent me home. My fears weren't over yet. First I was late for dinner, and then my mother would want to know why my dress was all rumpled. My mother told me not to be so late for dinner again and not to play so hard, my dress was a mess. It all ended well except for years after, I would wake up in the middle of the night with the fear of drowning.

I don't remember how old I was then, but I was under six. The summer I was six, I started *cheder*. No more playing in the lumber yard. *Cheder* lasted the whole day, or so it seemed to me. A cousin of my mother's first husband ran a *cheder* for beginning boys and girls and older boys. Girls didn't go any farther in school after they learned to read the prayer book. No one expected them to understand what they were reading. Her relative told my mother it was time for me to start *cheder*, and she agreed. To start school my mother made me a new dress. It was red silk. The only trouble was that it was made from a man's shirt. My mother had bought it from a neighbor; it was made too small for him. It had a stand up collar that buttoned on the side, the Russian way. That was the style of men's shirts. My mother made the sleeves and other parts to fit me, but she left the collar and opening as it was. I was in torment. The dress was everything I could wish for, bright red silk, but I was ashamed to wear it. I felt that everyone would know that it was made from a man's shirt and laugh at me. I complained, but was made to wear it anyway. Every morning I went to *cheder* with my arms crossed on my chest, hiding the side opening and collar.

Cheder was another torture. I think the manner of teaching is still in existence. When I was last in Israel I passed by a house where I heard children answering a question in unison. My *cheder* consisted of a room, not too large, with three long tables that had benches on both sides. Children crowded together on the benches, pushing one another. The *melamed* (teacher), my mother's relative, did not talk to us. He was teaching the older boys in another room. We had two or three young men teaching us; they were called "belfers." The belfers had pointers in their hands that were often used to hit a child over the head, face, or knuckles if he did not shout loud enough. The din was unbelievable, the air stuffy. I would come out of school felling dizzy, not knowing which way to turn for home.

The first table was for beginners, the second for the ones who could put the letters together, and the third for those who could really read. I never made the third table. I got sick and was sick for a long time. After I got well, I didn't go back to *cheder*.

When Purim came we children were very excited.[1] Purim is a joyous Jewish holiday celebrating Queen Esther's bravery in saving the Jewish people from the king's wicked advisor, Haman. There was a custom for friends and relatives to send each other sweets on that day. For that purpose a man was hired to carry the *shalachmanes*. He came carrying a big tray covered with a snow white cloth. There is a Yiddish saying, "That man makes a lot of money; he is a *shalachmanes* carrier." It was meant in derision. Though the man may have been well paid, Purim comes but once a year.

We would stand by the window and wait for his coming. We could hardly contain ourselves for joy when he knocked on the door. After the goodies were put on the table and the man left, we could have our fill of sweets. My joy was over; there weren't any of the sweets I wanted. I didn't like candy, cookies, or tortes.

Mother used to give us *groschens* (pennies to you) to go to the corner store to buy candy. We would troop down to the store, and my brother and sister would make their selection. I sadly looked on and would come home with the money still in my hand.

The Russian army occupied my part of Poland in those days. I don't know what other food the army got, but bread was issued to the soldiers once or twice a month. I really can't remember how often. The bread could not be bought in a store; however, the soldiers were very happy to exchange it for fine white bread. This had to be done in secret; they weren't allowed to exchange it. I guess it would break discipline. There were always a lot of soldiers on the streets, and when you saw one carrying a loaf of bread under his arm, that was the one to talk to. I grew up as many Jewish children in Brest-Litovsk did: speaking Russian, Polish, and Yiddish. Russian when playing with the Russian children, Polish with the Polish children, and Yiddish with the Jewish children.

The bread wasn't wrapped. As far as I can remember, the only thing that was wrapped in those days was French candy. The bread was from the whole rye grain with the chaff and bran included. The flour was coarsely milled, and the bread was very dark, lumpy, and heavy. That bread with sweet butter and sour apples was my steady diet.

In the evening my mother insisted I eat a regular meal. She would bring a plate of soup for each of us and go into the kitchen for something else. I would quickly eat my soup and Mollie's and Moshe's; they would return the favor by eating my meat. Sometimes Mother would catch us playing musical plates. They would have to eat the hateful soup, and I would choke on the meat.

Once my mother sent me to the store for vinegar. You brought the bottle with you, and the grocer filled it from a barrel. Our bottle had been used for that purpose many times; the cork didn't fit the bottle too tightly. On the way home I sat down on the sidewalk, opened the bottle, and began to drink the vinegar. It was strong, and I took one delicious sip at a time. That took a long, long time. When more than half the vinegar was gone, I realized I had been away too long, and I had very little vinegar left. I walked home slowly thinking what lie to tell my mother. I told her I fell down, and the vinegar spilled. For some reason, she didn't believe me. She wanted me to go back with her and show her where it happened. Since there wasn't a wet spot on the one block between our house and the store, I told her the truth. She then became concerned about my health; she thought I would burn up from so much vinegar. I told her I was fine; nothing hurt me. In later years, I would explain my poor singing voice by blaming it on the vinegar.

To get apples for me my mother went to a farmer who grew very sour apples in a village near the city. Once coming home with my mother after getting apples, I felt tired quite close to the house. I felt I couldn't make another step. I asked my mother to carry me. She said I was too big a girl for such nonsense. I can still see myself dragging my legs the last half block to our house, and that is all I remember.

The next thing I remember is lying in bed. I heard a lot of people around me, but I couldn't see them. I had come down with the measles, and they had settled in my eyes. I was told I had been sick for a very long time. My mother was crying for happiness that I was at least conscious and able to talk. The doctor came several times and prescribed something, but it didn't help. I couldn't lift my eyelids. I don't know if it was because I was weak or because I was blind, but I stayed in bed all the time. I was asked what I would like to have to play with. I asked for a ball. I could bounce it against the wall. A doll I couldn't see, I didn't want.

Cipha and her mother came to visit me after the danger of contagion was over. Cipha would sit at the other end of my bed, and we would throw the ball at one another. I missed catching it too many times; it wasn't fun. One morning I woke up and was able to raise one eyelid just a little. The first thing I did was feel around for my ball. I was told the ball had beautiful pictures painted on it. I made everyone tell me about the pictures again and again. Now, I could see them for myself.

In a few days, perhaps a week, I was able to raise both eyelids. My mother carried me to a chair by the window, and I looked at the snow that covered everything in sight. It surprised me that there was so much snow. The day I got sick it was warm; I wore no coat or sweater. I realized I had been sick for a long time.

I must have been about seven or eight years old when the cinema came to town. I remember the name of the place where the movies were shown; it was called "Fantasia." Mother took us to see the new wonder. The Fantasia was on the Nevsky Prospect, the main street of the city with fancy shops and restaurants.

The Nevsky Prospect was really three streets running parallel to one another. First there was the cobbled highway on which wagons or *droshkys* came in or left town. Then there was the dirt road for local traffic. After this was an esplanade with trees and benches on both sides. At intervals were kiosks where one could buy newspapers, magazines, and candy. Between this and the wide sidewalk was the third road. On this road *droshkys* would pull up in front of a shop or restaurant and beautifully dressed ladies would come out. Sometimes an officer in a splendid uniform was by their sides.

But let's get back to Fantasia. It was upstairs. One walked up a flight of stairs and entered a large red carpeted room. At a table sat a woman who sold tickets for the next performance. One didn't go in during the middle of a show. There were easy chairs and sofas all around, also a few small tables with chairs around them where tea was served. The price for the show wasn't all the same. Some tickets were higher than others. The closer one sat to the screen, the higher the price. That is understandable, for the chairs were on a flat surface, and the people in front would obscure the small screen. After the show Mother took us to a *conditorie*. That is the name that sticks in my mind of the shop where French pastries were sold. We had pastries and hot chocolate. These were the first sweets I liked. They were light, flaky, with lots of whipped cream on them. I told myself that when I grew up I would have a lot of these pastries. Alas, I never did again. In restaurants in America I would always try the French pastries, but it wasn't the same.

After my father moved to Warsaw (evidently my grandmother moved with him, for I never saw her again), I had no relatives in Brest-Litovsk other than my mother, sister, and brother. My sister and brother had uncles and aunts galore. On holidays my mother dressed them up and sent them to pay their respects to their relatives. There were some aunts and uncles who accepted me as a part of their family, the cousin who ran the *cheder* we called a "good" uncle, but there were others who said I was no relative of theirs. To these my mother sent only my brother and sister. I was made to stay home. I didn't know why I was so punished. I would cry very hard, lie on the floor, and kick, and bang my head. I was too young to understand why my sister and brother's uncles weren't my uncles too. Mollie and Moshe would beg my mother to let me come along. First, they were sorry for me, and, second, I was a big help to them. I was the one to push forward to knock on the door and say "*Guten Yomtov.*"[2] After the ice was broken, it was easier for them to follow. But my carrying on and their begging didn't help.

When they left in their finery I pretended to go out to play, but I didn't. I followed them at a distance until they came to where they were going. If they happened to look back, I would hide behind a tree or put myself flat against a building. When they came to their uncle's house they would start pushing one another, for they were too bashful to be the first one to knock on the door. I would hide myself behind a bush and cry for being so unlucky as not to have an uncle. When they came out, I would let myself be known, and we would walk home together. They would tell me it wasn't much fun, and I didn't miss anything. But my heart was heavy. I hated to be left out.

To the "good" uncles, sometimes Mother herself would take us, but mostly the three of us would be dressed up and sent on our own. Now that I have mentioned the "good" uncle who ran the *cheder*, my heart goes out to his memory. He was the kindest man I ever knew. He treated me as if I, too, was his cousin's child. I loved that man. I must tell how he looked. He was tall with blond hair and beard and kind, blue eyes. He wasn't just tall to a child's eyes; I could compare him to the other uncles who sometimes came to visit my mother on holidays. I still have a picture of this good uncle's four children: two boys and two girls. I'm sorry to say the children looked like their mother. But in my mind's eye, I have a firm picture of that wonderful man.

In the spring of 1914 my mother and Cipha's decided to share the expense of a tutor to teach us to read Russian. I believe it was for twice a week, an hour a day. I knew the alphabet and could read simple words by the time the tutor was drafted.

Chapter Three

There was talk of war and then there was war. I remember the excitement when the "extras" started coming out two and three times a day. Sometimes they were on green paper, sometimes on pink. The regular newspapers were white. Papers weren't delivered to subscribers as they are now here. Boys would sell them on corners, but when the extras came out they would run around yelling, "Extra! Extra!" and everyone would run to buy one.

The news was always good until 1915. Notice was given that the population would have to leave the city because a big battle was expected. At the end of town was a large ammunition dump, and it was thought that the enemy would surely go after the dump. Leaving the city was for our own safety. Where to go and by what means, we weren't told. The trains couldn't be used for civilians; they carried troops to and from the front. When I say "trains," I don't mean fast, efficient vehicles. A train might pass once a day with soldiers. Sometimes it wouldn't even stop. When it did stop, it might stay there for hours because the road ahead wasn't clear.

I cannot tell of all the confusion, all the heartbreak, when people were told that they would have to leave their homes and everything they possessed and go to "nowhere." People ran around trying to buy a horse and wagon or even wheelbarrows—anything that could carry a little more than they could carry in their hands or on their backs.

Many hundreds, or I should say, thousands walked out of the city with just what they could carry on their person. We were the lucky ones. A cousin of my mother's first husband (he was another "good" uncle to me) had a brewery. He therefore had horses and wagons. He gave a wagon and horse to one of his drivers to take the driver's family and ours out of the city. I don't remember what time limit was given for the people to leave their homes. It must not have been very long, a month or two. Whatever length, we all had to go.

The man came to pick us up. The wagon was already loaded with all his portable goods, his wife, and his many children. There was still plenty of room for our belongings; we even took along an iron folding bed. My great sorrow was that I couldn't take my cat with me. My mother felt sorry about that too, but she said that the cat would be better off. The door of the house would be left ajar so that she would have a place to stay, and she would find food on her own. Everybody left their doors open. Who would steal anything? If they did, it didn't matter.

The wagon was finally loaded to the brim. We all sat on top of the baggage. It wasn't comfortable and it wasn't safe. We had to hold on to each other or to the heavier things around us so we wouldn't fall off. We were leaving the city. At first we were on the cobbled highway; a few miles out of town, it was a rutted dirt road. We weren't alone; there were other wagons and people on foot carrying the little they could take with them, and their children trailed after them. This mode of transportation wasn't a speedy one. Even in our wagon we didn't travel much faster than the people walking.

We came to a spot where workmen were smoothing the road with a mechanized roller. We had never seen one. It was a wonder to us, and a big surprise to our horse. He reared and almost turned over the wagon. After this the driver walked in front of the horse and led him until we had passed all the machinery. No one knew where to go. Where there was a fork in the road some people took it. Some families became separated and never found each other again. After the war societies were set up to try and find the lost children. Many weren't found. Either they were dead or didn't remember who they were.

Late in the afternoon just before sundown we would pull off the road near the closest village or town. The horse was tired and needed to be fed. The people too were tired and hungry. When one wagon pulled off the road, many others did too, though some went on. The farther we went, the smaller the crowd became. Wood was gathered and fires were made. There were always fallen branches and, if not, wooden fences were torn down. The villages were already empty. The peasants left their crops in the fields and fled. Potatoes roasted in ashes and dry bread was our diet. How long we were on the road, I don't remember. The days were so alike, they made no impression on me.

Finally we came to a town where the people said they would take into their homes anyone who wanted to stay or as many as they could accommodate. The Jews took in Jews; the Gentiles took in Gentiles. My mother decided to stay. The driver of our wagon and his family went on, and we never saw them again. We were taken in by a family who had two daughters, one as old as my sister, the other somewhat younger. The house consisted of two rooms. In the first room was a large brick oven in which the cooking was done. The side of the oven was extended into a flat space; on that space the four of us slept. That was the warmest spot in the house; there was no other heating. The kind family that shared their house with us slept in the next room. I think we were more comfortable.

We stayed there a few weeks; then a one room cabin was found for us. This too had an oven on which we all slept. There was no other thing to sleep on. There were just two or three wooden benches and a narrow wooded table that was evidently made by the peasant who lived there, but who fled in fear of the Germans.

Moshe and I were given the job of going to the forest nearby to collect fallen branches and saw them into the proper size to fit the oven. Winter was coming. We needed a lot of wood to cook with and to keep the cabin warm. We piled up row upon row of wood against the back wall. Mother said it would last us for two winters. My brother and I were very proud of the good job we did and so sad when we had to leave it.

After all the preparation the Russian high command made to defend Brest-Litovsk, the city was easily taken by the Germans. In fact, there wasn't even a battle. The Germans came in through a different road than was expected. As the Russians fled, they set fire to the city. But they didn't have much time, only half of the city was burned. That is what the German soldiers told us when they came to the town we were in. A few years later when we came back to Brest-Litovsk, half of the city was burned and the other half not.

The night before the Germans came we heard shouting, and some houses at the end of town were set on fire. The next morning the Germans just walked in. They came in good will, they told us. They gave candy to the children and cigarettes to the men. This was in the early fall. By midwinter notices were put up on posts, and people in the streets told that if they were not inhabitants of the town, only refugees, they would have to leave. We were also told we would be taken to a nicer place with better housing and plenty of food.

Knowing a Russian winter, no one wanted to travel in it. We all claimed to have lived there for years. A new plan was devised. All people, including children of any age, seen on the street were to be locked up. Notices again were posted that if members of your family had been imprisoned, you had to bring proof that you had lived in the town at least two years, and then they would be released. If you had no proof, you should pack up your belongings, dump them in the town square, and join those in detention. The belongings would be safe, we were assured, because soldiers would be stationed to watch them. Two or three assigned personnel would also come to each house to ask for proof of residence. If proof could not be given, that family was to be locked up too.

We lived at the very end of town. By the time they came to our house, we had already heard what was happening. One of us would always sit by the window to watch for their coming. When they were in sight, we would all go up the attic. We would lie in the dusty straw until the knocking stopped and a little longer, just to be sure.

But all this didn't work. We needed to go out to get food. Moshe was sent out to get food, a loaf of bread. A devious route was worked out so he wouldn't be seen. He was seen and locked up. When my brother didn't come home after a few hours, we packed up our belongings and went to join him. The iron folding bed was left in the cottage as payment for rent to the peasant in whose house we had lived for several months.

Our joining my brother was a sad beginning for what followed. Only my mother was able to see him just for a few minutes to show her he really was there. Men and women were separated. There were empty rooms except for rows of bunks on top of one another. That is where we slept and waited. I don't remember how long, maybe a week. Then a long train of wagons came for us. The belongings from the square were piled into them. We were to sit on top of that.

We started up. It was bitter cold, and the snow was deep. Adults preferred to walk beside the wagons to keep warm. Toward evening we came into a snowstorm. We kept right on going. Not really going though, very often the whole train had to stop, for the first wagon lost the road. The driver would call to us in back to help him find the road. All the time it was snowing with the wind driving it into our faces. I was sitting on the wagon while my mother and sister and brother were waking beside it. I was so numbed with cold, I couldn't feel anything. The wagon lurched, and I fell off. I wasn't hurt, but I made no effort to call out or move. I was past caring what happened to me. In the blizzard my mother didn't notice that I wasn't on the wagon. Then I heard her yell, "Stop! My child is lost!" She came running back to find me lying on the side of the road, bunched up as I fell.

Toward morning we came to a rail track where boxcars were waiting for us. We were told to get into them—not merely told, we were pushed in. Standing room only, and not much of that. We were crowded shoulder to shoulder, back to back. One thing I can say about this method of packing us in, it soon got very hot. I, being so much smaller than anyone around me, got hardly any air at all, and I fainted. My mother got someone to roll back the door a little, got some snow, and rubbed my face with it. Later we found the only water we had to drink was the snow we could scrape off the outside of the boxcar; the only food, some dry bread. If someone didn't have any, it was shared and passed over head to head until it came to the needy one. To go to the bathroom we used chamber pots, standing up, where we were, in front of everyone, men and women together. It was humiliating, but what else could we do? Whenever the train stopped, we would open the doors and empty our pots. We were three days on the train.

On the third day around noon we came to a railroad station. A town could be seen in the distance. Our train stopped, but we weren't allowed to leave the cars or even to open the doors. When it got dark, we were told to come out and start walking. It was a three mile walk, but at the time we didn't know that. We also found out later why we weren't allowed to leave earlier. The powers that were, were afraid the people in town would rebel if they saw such a horde brought in. But the good people of Ostrolenka didn't feel like that at all. The road we walked on in the dark was lined with people. Everyone had something to give us, a piece of bread, a cookie, a piece of cake. Some even brought teapots, poured cups of tea to the passing crowd, and walked along with us as we drank, for we weren't allowed to stop. We had to take what was given to us on the go.

We finally reached our destination. Three miles out of Ostralenka was a small village. Towards the end of the village and to the left of the road in a clearing of the forest was a barracks, a training camp for the Prussian army. The floors of these barracks were lined with straw. It wasn't fresh straw; it was left over from the trainees. On that dusty dirty straw everyone flopped down, and that is how we spent our first night in our new haven.

The next day German efficiency began to work. Every man, woman, and child was put to work to pick up the straw, to sweep the place clean, and to wash the floors. I don't think there were any complaints. Everyone was glad to have something to do after the three miserable days in the boxcars. Food was distributed, potatoes and bread. A certain amount was given to each family. Evidently, there was enough; I don't remember going hungry while we were in the barracks. Fires were made outside to cook the potatoes.

At the end of the barracks a dispensary was set up with several doctors. People needed to be treated for the frostbite from the night we were taken to the boxcars. Some cases were bad; toes, and sometimes a leg, had to be amputated.

In the rest of the barracks double bunks were set up. My brother and sister slept on the upper ones; my mother and I on the lower ones. I so much wanted to sleep on an upper bunk, but my mother had enough of me falling out of places. The sexes weren't separated, and the only privacy was the dark.

Our belongings were brought from the last town's square. We had a large trunk that was put at one end of our bunks. After a few days I didn't want to play with the other children. All I wanted was to lay on that trunk, close my eyes, and see beautiful scenes. I had no pain, and so there was no reason to complain to my mother. I liked the state I was in. One day a man passed by and asked my mother why I was always lying on the trunk. She told him that was my way of playing. He felt my head and it was hot. He told my mother I had a fever, and she felt my head. Then she became concerned about me, and took me to the dispensary. By that time I couldn't walk, and she had to carry me. I didn't know what was wrong with me, but in a few days I got better and could no longer see the beautiful pictures when I closed my eyes.

We were in the barracks a couple of months. I don't know what happened to all the people that were with us. They must have been taken some place else, for only a few families found housing in the village. Perhaps they went to the town. We found a log cabin that stood in the middle of a wheat field. There was a long narrow walk to the road through the field.

In the spring just before Passover my sister got sick. A doctor was called. He told my mother that Mollie had typhus fever. She was taken to the hospital in town three miles away. In a few days I joined my sister in a bed right next to hers. Mother came to see us every day. After twelve days my mother stopped coming. Each day we would look for her, but she didn't come. Two days later my mother was brought in and put in a bed opposite to us. She was delirious and didn't know us. My sister was told she would have to help take care of my mother. I was given my clothes and told to go home. I was better, and there weren't enough beds for the really sick ones.

The hospital was a long wooden building on the same side of town as our village, but it was three miles to our house. I got dressed and made it to the steps outside and had to sit down again. It took about five hours of alternate walking and resting before I stumbled into our cabin. Moshe was sitting alone in the dark crying. He was sixteen, five years older than I; he wasn't crying because he was afraid of the dark. He saw how tired I was and said only a few words to me. He asked me if I was hungry. I told him I had nothing to eat that day. He said there was half a *ma'zah* I could have; it was the last day of Passover.[3] There was nothing else in the house. I ate the *matzah* and went to bed.

Two days later a neighbor came to our cabin to tell us she had just come from the hospital. My mother died that morning. My brother was to go to town right away for the funeral which was to be held that afternoon. He left, and I was by myself. I was still too weak to walk the three miles to the hospital. I cried a little, but I did not believe what the woman told us. I said to myself: it can not be true, it was all a mistake. My mother can not die and leave her children helpless, without family, without friends, without money. She can not die, for she loved my brother, her only son too much. She can not die. She can not die. Some other woman must have died, and they thought it was my mother. I was sure my brother would come back soon and tell me it wasn't our mother who died. In the evening both Moshe and Mollie came home. There wasn't much talk; we just cried. We sat *shiva*, but all the time in my heart I knew my mother was still alive.[4] In the village, or once in a while when I would go into town, if I saw a dark-haired woman the same size as my mother, I would run in front of her to look into her face—this could be my mother. I never found her.

The night my mother died, I wet my bed. I was eleven. It was the first time in my sister's memory since I was three. I wet my bed every night. My sister washed the sheets every morning. In the big house near the road lived a family who had a girl about my age. That summer the mother told my sister that I am invited to a sleep-over party for her daughter's birthday. Sheets will be spread on the grass, and we will sleep outside. I refused to go; if I wet my sheet, I will never be able to look into anyone's face. My sister said that if I feel that bad about wetting my bed, I will be very careful and will surely not wet that night, and that may stop me from wetting forever. I gave in and went to the party. When I woke up in the morning, my sheet was wet. I ran straight home. The girl's mother came to complain to my sister and show her my sheet. She said a girl of eleven should not wet her bed; it was my sister's fault, she isn't bringing me up right. She said I ruined her sheets. My sister said she will wash and iron the sheets and bring them back clean. I wanted to bury myself in the ground.

I eventually stopped wetting my bed, but I never stopped turning after women with dark hair to look into their face to be sure it wasn't my mother. My youngest son once asked me if I feel sorry for myself for what happened to me in the past. But I am not that little girl anymore. She and I are eons apart though I can see her in my mind's eye, remember her thoughts, her grief. No, I don't feel sorry for myself, but I feel sorry for that little girl.

Chapter Four

After we left the barracks, they were used as a rest home for soldiers weary from battle. A company of soldiers would march in, stay a week or two, leave, and another company would come in. There was a regular staff of men who were there all the three years that we lived in the village. They were older men; I suppose that is why they were selected for the job. The village was small. The regulars and the villagers got to know each other.

Yiddish and German are similar languages. The Jews could make themselves understood to the soldiers in Yiddish and translated for the Russians and the Poles. The soldiers were kind to everyone, especially to children. They would pat us on the head, give us candy, and ask how old we were. They would tell us that they too had children at home younger or older than we were. I remember one particular soldier. He was a short dark man. His name was Fritz Stein. He told us he had ten children, and some of his sons were at the front. Many times tears would come into his eyes when he talked about his family. It was easy to talk to the children in the village. We always played in the middle of the road.

Times were hard for all the people around us, but they were worse for us. We ran out of money, and there was no employment for my sister or my brother. The soldiers wore fatigues and did their own laundry, but the officers always had on white shirts. Mollie went to ask if she could do their shirts for them. A few agreed to let her do the shirts if she washed them very clean. After a trial, they were satisfied with her work. My sister had to wash the shirts by hand with a bar of yellow soap because there weren't any washing powders. We had a wooden washtub and a corrugated wash board. Mollie would soap the shirts, scrub them on the board, rinse them, and then re-soap them and let them soak overnight in the tub. The water had to be carried from a well about a hundred feet away. That was my job.

Moshe went to farmers miles away to ask for work. One hired him. The farm was seven miles away. Every morning my brother would get up at 4:30 and go to his job. After working all day, he would walk the seven miles back home again. He would come home after dark very tired. He would eat a few boiled potatoes with a piece of bread and go to sleep.

We lived in a one room cabin. Mollie and I slept on the oven, Moshe on the floor on a mattress made of straw. One day my brother came home from work very late. My sister and I were asleep. He came into the dark house, took off his coat, put it on the nearest thing to him, and went to sleep. In the morning was tragedy. He had put his coat on the tub where the shirts were soaking. All the shirts were a deep blue. The heart-rendering cries of my sister, the remorse of my brother—how can I tell of it and give it justice?

It meant complete starvation. Even with their earnings we were hungry, for often there was no food to buy. We ate once a day. In the evenings only we had a few potatoes and sometimes a piece of bread. Now we would have no food and no money. My sister would somehow have to pay for those shirts and would no longer be given any to wash. The officers didn't have too many shirts to have some of them ruined. At one end of the village lived a young Polish woman who also did washing for the officers. After hours of crying Mollie went to her to ask if there was anything that could be done about those shirts. The woman gave her a bottle of bleach, and told her to try soaking them in a strong solution of water and bleach. My sister didn't know bleach existed. The shirts came late to their owners, but they were as white as snow.

I would like to tell about the countryside. It was really a beautiful spot. On our side of the road there were fields, and across the road was forest. The forest ran for miles, but the density of the trees wasn't all the same. Across the road where our narrow walk ended were houses. Some of my friends lived there. I would go over to them, and we would go roaming among the trees and bushes looking for scattered strawberries and raspberries. The strawberry bushes were more plentiful; we only found two raspberry bushes. We ate the berries as we picked them.

There were clearings with all sorts of wild flowers. We didn't pick them, we just ran around chasing each other. Once I was by myself. I investigated a little farther to the left and I found a lake. It was a lonely spot. I took off my clothes and went into the water. That is where I learned to swim. There were a lot of fish in the water. I would try to catch them with my hands, but I couldn't. There were big yellow flowers floating on the lake. I picked one up, smelled it, and got very dizzy. I crawled out of the water and laid on the grass a long time before I could get dressed and go home.

On that side of the road to the right were more houses and then the barracks. After the barracks the forest started in earnest. There were no clearings, the trees were tall, their branches met at the top. One could barely see the sky. On the hottest day it was cool and dark underneath the trees. I didn't go there to keep cool. My job was to gather pine cones for fuel. I was careful never to lose sight of the road. I kept going farther and farther away, and the sack of pine cones became heavier each day I trudged home.

One day I decided to go just a bit deeper into the forest. I saw a lot of pine cones on the ground that I could gather. It wouldn't make my way home much longer, for I would only go twenty or thirty feet deeper into the woods than usual. I made all sorts of signs to find my way back to the road. In a few minutes I had a sackful of pine cones. I stood up and went back to where I thought the road was. No road. It was dark, cold, and frightening. At first I merely walked in every direction. I was barefooted and the pine needles pricked my feet; they were bleeding. Large ants crawled all over me. I dropped my sack of pine cones and started running, all the time yelling for help. Every child has heard of wolves and other wild animals in the woods. I didn't think that I would ever come out alive. In my yelling for help, I was also saying good-bye to my brother and my sister. I ran around for a good many hours; by that time my voice could barely be heard. All of a sudden I saw a peasant running towards me. I didn't know if he would kill me or save me, but it was good seeing another human being. I ran into his arms. He asked me what I was doing there, and I sobbed out my tale. He took me by the hand and led me to the road. I wasn't more than fifty feet from it, but I was a long way from home. I was no longer sent to gather pine cones.

In the evenings I would go to my friends. We would sit in the dark and tell each other ghost and witch stories until our skin crawled. From their house to the road wasn't too far, but from there on I had a long walk in empty fields, and it was pitch dark. I was sure a goblin would get me one of those nights. That didn't stop me from doing the same thing again and again. My friends would ask me if I was afraid to go home. I wouldn't admit to any such weakness.

We had electricity in our cabin. A long cord hung from the ceiling with a socket and a lonely bulb in it. One late afternoon my sister pulled the string that hung from the socket. The bulb flashed, and the light went out. Moshe wasn't home from work yet, and Mollie was busy washing and ironing. I was sent to get a light bulb. For that I had to walk three miles to town. I went, got the bulb, and started for home. As I left the town it was already dark. In the three miles between the town and my house there were two or three creeks crossing the road with wooden bridges over them. Everyone knows that witches and goblins live under bridges. I walked a while in the dark with my heart beating so I could hardly breathe. Then I came close to a bridge. I couldn't make another step. I stayed where I was and prayed to God to send someone going my way. Even if I saw someone going the other way, I thought I would quickly run across the bridge while they were crossing, and at the next bridge I would wait for another miracle. It was a lonely road, pitch dark, with no one going in either direction. I stood there for a long time, and then I heard a voice in back of me. It wasn't a witch. The voice spoke in German. Two soldiers came along the road. I immediately ran between them and stayed there until I turned off on the walk to our house. Every once in a while they would ask me why I was walking between them, but I pretended I didn't understand them.

There was no sort of amusement for the soldiers who came to rest or for the personnel who were there all of the time. Even in the town there were no movies or theatres. Someone fell on a plan to have a dance, and the whole village was to be invited, the children too. Of course the old men and women didn't go, and young men, there were none. But there were young married women and young girls like my sister, and they were delighted with the idea. I remember one young married woman in particular, first because I baby-sat with her little boy while she and her parents went to Yom Kippur services (my payment was a piece of bread with jelly on it—after the fast), and second because she had a green moiré evening gown that had a loop on the hem.[5] When she danced, the loop was on her finger and held up the train so it didn't drag on the floor. She was the only one who had anything so grand as an evening gown, but all the young women tried to spruce up too. They had dresses made by a dressmaker in town. My sister could only afford a new blouse. It was a beautiful blouse. It was white silk that had narrow green stripes running up and down.

The dance was a big success, and more dances were given at intervals. My only interest in those dances was the magician who was one of the permanent personnel. Sometime during the evening the dancing would stop, and he would perform magic for us. All I remember of this magic is that he pulled silver coins out of people's noses and ears while running a continuous patter. It must have been funny, for we all laughed. I remember the man; he was tall, blond, heavy-set, and almost completely bald.

Since our little house stood in wide fields, my sister undertook another source of income. She bought a few chicks. In the summer they could grub for themselves, and in the winter we would feed them. When they grew into chickens and laid eggs, we would sell the eggs. This enterprise was successful. Before long we had almost a dozen chickens. The eggs were all sold to the personnel at the barracks. We never ate the eggs ourselves.

My brother was in town on market day. A farmer sold him a bargain: a little black chicken for fifteen *groschen*. It was a big bargain, for a chicken was worth three times that much even if it was young and didn't lay eggs yet. But one look at that scrawny black thing, and you knew it was no bargain. My brother admitted that he bought it because he felt sorry for it. The other chickens picked on it. When they were fed, they wouldn't let it come near the food.

I named it Maeshele after my brother whose nick-name was Maeshe. The "le" is a diminutive in Yiddish. I would throw the feed to the other chickens, step aside, and "Maeshele, Maeshele," and it would come running to my very feet to be fed. It became so used to its name, no matter how far it roamed, when I called it, it came running. When the time came we had to leave the village, I was heartbroken over my pet. I knew whoever bought our chickens wouldn't keep Maeshele for her eggs; she would be the first one to go into the pot. For years I didn't eat chicken. I always saw little black Maeshele before my eyes.

There was a shortage of all raw material, but leather for shoes was the worst. When our shoes gave out, there was no replacing them. If one had a lot of money, one could buy black market shoes. The soles were made out of machinery belts. But it was illegal to strip the idle machinery of its belts. Evidently, the Germans thought they would keep what they had won so far in battle and wanted to preserve such important things as machinery. Shoes like that were too dear for us to buy. Moshe was clever with his hands, and he made wooden clogs for the three of us like the ones worn nowadays. But my brother's were better; he put hinges in the soles, and they would bend as he walked.

We were always hungry. Food wasn't rationed, but it cost a lot. We never had enough money to buy food to satisfy our hunger. In the morning we would have a slice of bread with margarine and in the evening, potatoes. The bread was measured, an exact slice for each of us; the potatoes were counted onto three plates.

We had a baker in the village, but he didn't always have flour to bake bread. When he did get some flour, he would let people know, and there would be bread the next day. Once I went for the bread. It was a small round loaf of rye bread. The aroma of fresh baked bread is delicious, and the bread was still warm. On the way home I broke off a small piece, and I was so hungry, I ate it. After that I couldn't stop breaking off one piece after another. By the time I got home only half a loaf was left. My sister was furious with me. The bread was supposed to last a week for the three of us.

There came a time when the baker couldn't get any flour at all. The officials in the barracks put out a notice that anyone who wanted could come to the barrack's kitchen at noon and get soup, the same as was given the soldiers. I went to the barracks with a blue metal pitcher and stood in line with the other people. There was banter and joking between the people in line and the soldiers. My pitcher was filled to the brim. The soup was rich with meat and vegetables. It was delicious, but it wasn't kosher. My brother reasoned with the law: if we didn't eat the soup, we would be starving; a Jew must preserve his life; therefore, we could eat the soup—but not the meat. We carefully picked out the meat and threw it away. Not for long did we have a problem with the meat. Soon there was no meat in the soup, and it became thinner and thinner until there was nothing in it but a few pieces of potato and free floating oatmeal flakes. There was no more jolly talk between the people and the soldiers. In silence we would get our watery soup, and in silence we would go home with it.

To me it seemed that we were in that village for half a lifetime, but we were there only three years. We were told that the war was over and we could go home. We were glad to go, but we were sad also. We were leaving our mother behind in an unmarked grave, and we had no home to go to. When my sister and I were in America, my brother had a stone put on my mother's grave and had his picture taken standing by the stone and sent it to us.

Chapter Five

The authorities provided a train to take the refugees back to their home cities. We found a three room flat on the other side of Brest-Litovsk from where we used to live. My one burning wish was to go to the house where we used to live, where I was born. I went there but found nothing but a heap of rubble and charred trees.

The farmers sowed their fields, and when the fighting started between the Bolsheviks and the newly formed Polish government, they left their homes, for most of the fighting was at first in the country. The Red Army was beaten back. For a while there wasn't any shooting. The crops were ready for harvest, and some of the farmers hadn't come back yet. A smart entrepreneur decided it was a good thing. He put out a handwritten notice and posted it on a telephone pole in the main street. It said that he needed people to dig up potatoes, and he would pay in kind. All who were interested should be there Monday morning.

Food was hard to come by even if one had money, and we didn't have any. I showed up with a little basket with the rest of the women. At first the man wouldn't let me come along. I was too small and skinny for the work he told me. After crying and begging I was allowed to go along. There was no food in the house, and so, of course, I had no breakfast. I don't think that any of the people there had anything to eat that morning. He led us out into the fields, and we dug potatoes. He told us to us to dig deep to be sure we got all the potatoes out.

Sometime before noon he had some of us pick up wood, broken branches, anything that would burn. He made a fire and put in potatoes to roast. That was to be our lunch and part payment for our labor. Not too much time was given for us to straighten our backs or rest, and we were back to work. We worked until sundown and then we lined up to be paid for our day's work. I didn't get paid too many potatoes; after all I was the littlest and didn't deserve as much pay as the grown-up women. It didn't matter. By that time, I couldn't carry much anyway. But I did bring home enough for my brother's and sister's dinner.

In a few days we had dug up all the potatoes in that area. He then led us farther afield. It was always hard for me to keep up with the rest of the women on the way home. I straggled behind, but when we came to the edge of town, they were still in sight, and after reaching the town, it didn't matter. But this field was much farther away. On my first going home carrying my little basket with perhaps five pounds of potatoes, I kept falling farther and farther behind. I didn't like it, but soon the rest of the company was entirely out of sight. The sky was darkening. I was getting cold, and I was so tired, I could hardly put one foot in front of the other. As I was walking on this lonely dirt road, I was very much afraid. On the left side of the road, I saw a little wooden cottage. I was afraid to come near it, but there was no other way for me to go home. As I came near, the door opened, and a soldier with a rifle in hand came out. He told me to stop. He came over and looked in my basket. He took it off my arm and walked back into the cottage. I felt so sad about losing my potatoes after so many hours hard work, and coming home empty-handed, I laid down on the ground and cried. I had eaten in the field, but my basket contained the only food my brother and sister would have that day. I cried a long time. I finally dragged myself home. My sister was frantic. Everybody was home from the potato fields for hours. She wanted to know what happened to me. I told her and then collapsed on the floor. I was sick for more than a week. There was no more potato digging for me.

The Red Army came back and started fighting in earnest around our city. Bombs were dropped and bullets were flying over our heads. I don't think either army had enough ammunition to put up a constant fight. Shooting started at four in the afternoon and lasted until dark. There was a plum tree in a yard across the street from where we lived. I would climb the tree, sit out on a branch, and try to reach out and eat the plums. One day the planes came early. I climbed down when I heard them and started running for home. An old woman running next to me was strafed and fell to the street. I kept running. Another time I saw a soldier with a bare bayonet on the street. I started running away from him, and he ran after me. I ran to the nearest door, knocked, and begged to be let in. No one answered. I knew people were inside; I could hear them whispering. Close by was a big crater in the ground made by a bomb a few days ago. I rolled into it and lay flat on the ground. To this day I am surprised the soldier didn't see me. He also knocked on the same door, and when there was no answer, he went away.

I so much wanted to live. My thoughts were always occupied with where to run, where to hide. To live one more day, one more day. There was no safety even in your own home. One day my sister left the house. She told me to lock myself in and not to open the door to anyone. Just after she left, there was a knock on the door. I thought my sister had forgotten something and came back. I was about to open the door, but first I looked through the kitchen window to make sure it was her. It was a soldier. I ran into the next room and hid under a bed. The knocking stopped after awhile. Then I heard knocking on the door of the apartment adjoining ours. The door was opened. I soon heard the screams of the man, woman, and their two year old child as they were being murdered. I don't have to say, I still hear those screams.

Finally the fighting around our city stopped, and the soldiers left. We were free to walk the streets again. More and more people came back home but none of our relatives, not the good uncles nor the bad. We never saw them again.

The better educated young Jewish people became concerned about the children who, during the war years, had no chance to learn to read or write. My own education consisted of knowing the Russian and Hebrew alphabet, and I was able to read and write a few simple words in each language. In Russian I understood what I read, in Hebrew, I didn't. Girls were only taught to read prayers, not to understand them.

The concerned people got together, and each was to teach what he knew best. Others went around town asking people to donate books for a library. One young man began to teach us Hebrew. He must have been a very good teacher. In a short while I learned to read Hebrew well and to understand what I read. At home I would only talk Hebrew to my brother. It annoyed my sister; though she could read Hebrew, she couldn't understand a word we were saying.

We were now under Polish rule. The important language was the one of the people we were governed by. A Polish officer undertook to teach us Polish. It seems none of the other children had lived in a mixed neighborhood before the war. I was the only one who could speak Polish. The officer of course couldn't talk Yiddish. I was in my glory. I was often called on to explain what he said. I fell madly in love with him. I meant to grow up to be a great beauty, not the dark, skinny thing I really was. When I will become beautiful, I thought, he will take one look at me and fall in love with me. What a happy ending.

There was one class I hated, for I didn't know anything about the subject. That was arithmetic. There were children who could do fractions; I didn't know what the answer was to even three times nine.

The books that were donated made a small library. That library was my joy. I read *Sherlock Holmes*. I cried over *Uncle Tom's Cabin*. I read Jack London (I meant to look him up when I got to America). I read *The Three Musketeers, The Count of Monte Cristo*, and several volumes of Balzac (it was one continuous tale, and I never found out how it ended because the rest of the volumes were missing). All these books were in the Yiddish translation. Your Uncle Stanley's standing joke is, "My mother has read everything in the original Yiddish."

Societies were set up in different cities. People who were looking for their lost ones could write to them. The society would put up a list of names in some prominent part of the city of the people who were being looked for. One day my mother's name was on the list. My father was looking for my mother.

My sister got my father's address from the society (we had lost his address in our travels), and wrote to him of my mother's death. In a short time we received a letter from my father with a check for fifty dollars. He wrote that he wanted his daughter and also Mollie and Moshe, the children of his wife, to come to him, and he would care for them as his own. He would send tickets for the three of us. My sister was to start getting papers and passports ready.

I don't know the exchange value of the American dollar to the then Polish *zloty*, but we felt like veritable millionaires. A few weeks later another check for fifty dollars arrived. My sister started to work on getting passports for us, but there was one fly in the ointment. Moshe was of military age and couldn't leave the country. My sister wrote that to my father. He sent tickets for me and Mollie. Moshe would have to wait until such time as he could come too.

After several trips to Warsaw, for we had no papers to show that we had ever been born, my sister got passports for the two of us. Now came the time to say good-bye to my brother. I cannot describe the sadness in our hearts when the train pulled out and my brother was left standing alone on the platform. When I looked at him I thought, "It is not possible I will never see Moshe again." We kept telling each other that in a few years he would come to America too, but even the few years that we would have to wait to see him seemed too long.

We never saw our brother again. By the time that he had fulfilled his military service and could come, a quota had been put on immigration to America. Since Moshe was not my father's son, he had to go on a waiting list. It might be fifteen or twenty years before his number came up.

He could not find work in Poland. He went into Russian territory a few miles away because it was said that anyone who wanted to work would not starve there. Somehow he got to Argentina. He wrote us from there for a while. Then he wrote that he had no work and no money and he was going back to Russia with some friends. He went to Berabejan (I don't know how to spell it in English). We corresponded often; we knew what he did and where he was until 1939, then complete silence. He had married; in the last letter I got from him was a picture of his nine month old daughter. That was the last we heard from our brother with whom we'd suffered so much. We never knew if he'd been killed by Stalin or by the Nazis. My sister and I kept writing to him, but our letters weren't even returned. After the Second World War we searched for him and his wife and daughter through the societies and even hired a private investigator. It was just as if he'd never existed. I can still see Moshe waving good-bye to us as the train pulled out of Brest Litovsk. All the hunger and fear we shared, we couldn't share a happy moment together.

Our first stop was Warsaw. We were examined by doctors and told we were in good health and could go to America. We weren't the only ones going. There were long hours spent waiting our turn and anxiety in our hearts whether we would pass inspection.

The next stop was Danzig. From there we were to take a ship to London, and from London to America. We were again examined and passed inspection. We boarded the boat in Danzig, and on deck was another horde of doctors. My sister was examined first and she passed. My turn came, and after a long eye examination, an interpreter was called to tell that I couldn't go. I first must have an eye operation before I could go on the boat.[6]

What a terrible disappointment just when we thought we were near the end of our troubles. There were many people rejected for one reason or another—that is, for the time being. Wooden barracks were put up outside Danzig, again with bunks one on top of the other, and that is where my sister and I were to stay until my eyes were operated on.

We went to a doctor whose name we were given. He examined my eyes and told my sister that before he would operate on my eyes he would have to take out my tonsils. That would help my eyes to heal faster. He would do both operations. But I could only have an anesthetic for one operation because it wasn't safe for me to have an anesthetic for both. Mollie and I talked it over. There was really nothing to talk about. We wanted to get to America, and, as far as I could see, there was no other way.

The doctor said taking out my tonsils wasn't a big deal, and he could do it in his office. My sister was told to wait in another room. I was taken into the inner sanctum. He had a nurse with him, an old woman with very thick glasses. I was strapped into a chair, something like a dentist's chair. It could lean backwards. My hands and feet were tightly strapped. I couldn't move. He commenced to cut my tonsils. I couldn't scream. After the cutting was over, he heated a long rod over a gas flame. This instrument had a round disc at the end of it. When the disc was red hot, he put it down my throat to burn off any loose ends after the cutting. My throat was then sprayed with a terrible tasting, terrible smelling powder. I was unstrapped from the chair. I shot out of the room, past the room my sister was waiting in, wildly running into the street. I didn't know where I was running, and I didn't care. I wanted to run away from this terrible thing that happened to me. Mollie was running after me. My sister was nine years older than me. I was a skinny little thing, and at other times she could have caught me in a minute, but not this time. We ran for a long time until I finally tired, and Mollie caught up with me.

She took me back to the barracks and put me to bed. To ease my pain and as a treat, she bought some oranges for me. I tried to suck on them. For twenty years afterwards I couldn't eat an orange or drink orange juice. The pain and the taste and smell of that horrid powder would come back to me.

The following week I went to the hospital. My eyes were operated on. When I woke up from the anesthetic, I didn't feel much pain, just a smarting under the eyelids. Of course, my eyes were bandaged. I couldn't see, but I thought my troubles were over.

I wasn't in a room by myself. There were other patients who had eye operations. Their daily talk was of the fear of having to have the treatment of the "blue pencil." Some had it and some didn't. A new fear crept into my heart. I was telling God how much I had already suffered, and to spare me this last horror. The bandages were taken off, and the doctor said that I was getting along very well. One day he came in with a stick that looked like a pencil with a blue sharp tip at one end. He picked my eyelids up and ran the tip around my eyes. My eyes were on fire. My whole face became swollen. I was told I may or may not need that treatment again. God was on my side. I didn't need another treatment.

My eyes were swollen. I couldn't open them for a few days, but in time I was checked out of the hospital. We waited for the next boat to London. All told, we were in Danzig for six weeks. Part of the time was taken up with my operations; the rest of the time was waiting for a boat. So many people were going to America, they couldn't take us all at once. Finally we got on a boat. My eyes were examined again, and they passed inspection.

What a wonderful time we had on the boat. The sailors were all English, and we couldn't understand them, but their good humor and kindness didn't need an interpreter. They were always smiling and laughing. In the dining room were long tables. These tables were piled high with long platters of meat, spaghetti, potatoes, and other vegetables. The sailors waited on us, and by their motions we understood they were urging us to eat more. The meat was always mutton, my favorite. There were catsup bottles on the table, and we didn't know what it was. The sailors picked up the bottles and poured the catsup on the meat on our plates. It was delicious. Somehow, no one worried that the meat wasn't kosher.

I believe we were on the boat four days. It may have been longer; I don't remember. We reached London and were taken by a train to our hotel. At one time it was a regular hotel, but now it was given over to use by the immigrants. Everyone who was on the boat with us was in the hotel with us. Meals were supplied for us on the premises. I remember we got a lot of fish to eat. People began to complain about so much fish, but they complained to the women who served us, and they didn't understand us anyway.

In London I would walk only on the street our hotel was on. I was afraid to take any turns. I couldn't read the street signs nor could I ask my way back if I got lost. There was so much I wanted to see, yet I was like a prisoner tied to one street. Some people didn't even step out of the building.

One day I was looking out the window of the hotel, and a boy about my age stopped and said something to me. I didn't understand him. I answered him in Yiddish. I saw he didn't understand me. I tried Polish on him. Russian. His face was still blank. I tried Hebrew, and he answered me in Hebrew. I then walked out, and we had a nice long talk. A few days later he came back and said his parents wanted me and my sister to come to Friday night dinner. We accepted the invitation. On Friday the boy came and led us to his house. It was a very nice dinner, and Mollie could talk to his parents because they spoke Yiddish. I am sorry I don't remember the people's names. It made such a nice break for us to be with the people and to talk to someone from another country.

We were in London two weeks waiting for a boat to take us on the next step of our journey. It would be the last step for others, but not for us. We still had to go to St. Louis.

Finally we were put on a boat that was really going to America. It was a much larger boat than the one from Danzig to London. On the boat to London there were only immigrants; we all ate at a common table, and we all walked on the same decks. We were served by sailors who didn't ask us what we wanted—the food was put on the table; you took your choice. On this ship we were separated from the people we traveled with so far, with whom we sort of established a friendship, people we could talk to. Now we were surrounded by people whose language we didn't understand and who were dressed much better than us. But our troubles didn't end there. Our first meal on the ship was dinner. A man in a black jacket and bow tie came around and gave us a menu. We had never seen a menu before, but we understood we were to select our food from that. We couldn't read it. There were other people at our table, but we didn't know how to tell them we couldn't order. We thought we would listen to the other people and order the same thing, but it was hard to repeat what they said. My sister caught the word "potatoes." I could repeat the shorter word "bun." When the waiter took our order, Mollie said potatoes, and I said bun. The waiter looked a little surprised, but we knew we ordered what some people at the table did. The waiter came back with two plates of boiled potatoes and a plate of rolls.

That is what we ate the first night while we watched other people eating a good dinner. Next morning when we ordered the same thing, the waiter understood we couldn't read the menu. He brought us eggs, coffee, milk, jam, and assorted rolls.

My sister didn't enjoy her meals for very long. After a few days, she couldn't eat anything. She would lie on her bed and moan that she was dying. When the sea was completely calm, she would come up and eat something, but she would soon give it up—while I was roaming the deck, admiring the sea and the sky. It seemed such a wonderful thing that day after day there was no sight of land. I didn't know the sea could be that big.

Leona's parents, Pessie and Isadore Burstein, just after their wedding, 1904.

Leona running with a group of children among the ranks of soldiers near Ostrolenka.

Leona, age 14, sent this picture to her father just before she emigrated.

Leona (standing), Mollie, Moshe (second from the right), and three cousins in Europe

Moshe at Pessie Burstein's (their mother's) grave at a village near Ostrolenka in 1927.

Leona (center) in bright red silk Chinese pajamas at a slumber party with friends in St. Louis.

Leona, age 18, in New York.

Leona and Joe Tamarkin on their wedding day, June 15, 1930.

A four generation photograph taken in 1993: Leona Tamarkin, Pamela Tamarkin Reis, Elizabeth (Lizzie) Reis, and Leah Reis-Dennis

Chapter Six

Besides my sister being sick, there were other fears that haunted us. Rumor was always going around the immigrants that the last test was Ellis Island. Many people were sent back from the very shore of the country that was their last hope. Some even committed suicide. They had no place to go, and after all they went through to get that far, they had no will to live. I could be sent back; they might find my eyes were not good enough; it had happened before. I was examined by many doctors before, passed on, and then taken off the boat in Danzig. On Ellis Island they could be more particular.

Our fears were confirmed. When we arrived on Ellis Island we were again examined. The results weren't told to us. Every morning a list of names was read; those people whose names were read could leave that day. Day after day of waiting, our names weren't on the list. True, no one told us we would be sent back, but no one told us we could stay. To see the shore of the desired country and perhaps never to be able to walk on the streets of its cities, never to see my father and my brothers, only to go back to the miseries as before, was very hard to take.[7]

Just before the war, when she was seventeen, Mollie had fallen in love with our cousin. He went to America to make good. Since my mother, too, expected to come to America to rejoin my father, the understanding was that the young people would get married when we were united in the new land. Though our cousin didn't hear from us during the war years, he waited for my sister.

She wrote him from London on what boat she was sailing. When we came to Ellis Island he came to see us. He thought he would be able to show us the town for a few days. He would then put me on a train to St. Louis, and he and my sister would get married.

Our cousin wasn't allowed to see us. We could hear his voice in the next room and we yelled, "That's our cousin; we know him!" but the doors were kept locked. We couldn't get out and he couldn't get in. He came again the next day, and he brought us gifts. The gifts were given to us—two watches, one for each of us. Again we could hear his voice, but we couldn't see him.

We were kept there for ten miserable days. One morning our names were called; we were saved. It seems we were kept there so long because my father wasn't there to claim us, and no one else could bail us out. Only the person who had sent for us could do that. There was an organization of women, I believe they were volunteers, who concerned themselves with immigrants getting to the right places when their relatives couldn't come to Ellis Island to take them out. Since we had train tickets for St. Louis, my father was wondering why we had not arrived on schedule. He made inquiries and found out he had to authorize that organization to take us out. Until papers were signed and sent back and forth, we had to wait without knowing why.

A woman with a badge came for us and put us on a train. We understood that we were not to get off the train until we got to St. Louis. The woman tried to talk with us, but we didn't understand her. She spoke English, of course. We had no idea how long the trip would be and we had very little money left, just some coins that we didn't know the value of. After some hours the train stopped at a station. A young man came on carrying a basket with sandwiches. We saw people buying them. My sister put what coins she had on her palm; with the other hand she pointed at his basket. He took some coins and gave us two sandwiches. We didn't think he cheated us for other people watched the transaction. We sat in our seats through the night. The next morning another salesman got on the train. We knew we could buy food, but we didn't know if we had enough money left to pay for it. Mollie held out what was left—a dime and a nickel. The man took the nickel and gave us a candy bar. This time we thought we were being cheated because the man took the nickel instead of the dime; the dime was so much smaller. But no one watching said anything, and so we said nothing.

We got to St. Louis late in the afternoon. The conductor motioned us to get off. There was my father and my two brothers, Jacob and Albert, to greet us. I recognized my father but not my brothers. They were grown men now. Jake, the older of my brothers, was married and had a child a year old. His wife, Minnie, and daughter were there too. Minnie and I took a great liking to each other. We became good friends.

It was a happy party; at last we were really there. We went to my brother's place, for my sister-in-law prepared a meal for us. We traveled on a streetcar that rode on rails like a train. Later we took another streetcar to go home to my father's place. He lived in a three room flat on the corner of Ninth and Soulard on the first floor.

The next day my father went to work, and my sister and I were left to enjoy the freedom we came for. There wasn't too much traffic, but because we were on a corner, a car would pass once in a while. Cars in those days backfired often. Every time it happened, Mollie and I would quickly jump to find a place to hide. We thought we were being shot at as we were used to.

At first it was odd for me to call my father "Papa" as my brothers did. I had never called him anything except for the time he took me on his lap and gave me a coin to play with and the time he came to say good-bye before he left for America. In a few days I got used to calling him Papa, and it was very nice to have a father. I need no longer lie to friends about where my father was; he was right here.

A month came to an end. My sister was leaving to go back to New York and marry our cousin. My older brother, Jake, came to take her to the train. I was sitting outside on the porch and she passed me by. I looked the other way. She looked straight ahead. We couldn't say good-bye. I fell into a fit of crying after she left. Mollie wrote me that she cried all the way to New York. The three of us, Moshe, Mollie, and I had gone through so much together . Now we were all separated. It was good to be here, but I missed the ones I suffered with. I missed them very much.

When I was in St. Louis a short while I began to look at the people walking on the street. They all seemed so complacent. No one looked back to see if anyone was after them, they didn't seem afraid of being shot at. I was full of rage. How can people go so quietly about their lives when other humans are being torn to pieces? Once I saw a man dressed in rags walking around aimlessly. I knew he didn't know where his next meal was coming from. He, too, looked complacent. I was thinking of how many thousands would have liked to change places with me.

Twelve years later in 1933 I saw the fear I knew in my younger days, even here in America. A young woman rushed into my house (in those days I didn't keep the doors locked). She said, "Hide me. They're going to shoot me. They think I talked." I put her in a closet and went to the window to see who was after her. I thought it was a hoax. I saw a black car filled with men cruising by. They went up a block or two, and then started back. I saw it wasn't a hoax and soon they would be looking for her in the houses where they had lost sight of her. Since we lived in a corner house, my house would be first. In my mind I saw the girl, myself, and my ten month old son all being killed. I told the girl of my fears. She agreed that she wasn't safe in my house. She asked to go out by the back door so that she could run through my backyard from yard to yard and get away. I wanted to know what it was all about, but the girl was shaking with fear; there was no time to ask questions. The car went by a few more times, then disappeared. I often wondered what happened to the girl. I hope she got away.

Chapter Seven

My father had a sister and a brother in St. Louis. Both had grown and married children. My aunt, being the elder, had grandchildren about my age. Every Sunday we had visitors. Everyone came to see the cousin from Europe. Friends, too, came to visit once I was settled at my father's. One person who came to see me was the man who started the bakery my father worked for. He was Jewish; he came from Germany. He came to ask me about the old country. My father told me the way the bakery started. This man's wife baked very good rye bread. Her neighbors asked her to bake bread for them, and they would pay her. Before long she had so many customers, her husband had to deliver the bread in a horse and buggy. By the time I came, it was a much larger business, and the old man, Freund, only drove the horse and buggy for pleasure or as a means to get around.

When the bakery considered moving away from our street (they were only two blocks away), my father thought that they might move too far for him to get to work. He talked it over with me, and we both decided that he should quit working for the bakery and find a closer place to work. When the move of the bakery was completed and my father got a notice he can now come back to work, there was no talk between my father and me. He just told me he will be up at six o'clock the next morning and leave for the bakery soon after; I will have to fix my own breakfast.

Breakfast consisted of two eggs fried in a lot of butter, eaten with toast spread with butter, and a glass or two of milk. We both always had the same breakfast day in day out the first three years I lived with my father. Besides this nourishing breakfast, after I started to work, my father would fix my lunch: two kaiser rolls, well-buttered, with two scrambled eggs, lettuce, and a slice of tomato on each. I was to buy milk in a restaurant or the nearest grocery store. While I am talking about my father's diet for me, I might as well finish the whole day's eating. For dinner (day in and day out) my father would cook a thick barley soup with lima beans, onion, and about two pounds of kosher soup meat on the bone.

My father was always a thin man. Thirty years later when he died, he was still a thin man. My father stayed lean, but I grew to barrel size. I had no knowledge of calories or any food fads. I was hungry for so many years that what my father fed me I ate. The time came that even my father noticed that I was growing in width but not in height. We talked it over and decided to go to the doctor to find out why I am so fat. The doctor was an old man, I think older than my father. When he heard how much food I ate in a day, I think he was surprised I am still alive. He put me on a diet; my father was sure I would die from it. I didn't die but I lost a lot of myself. I know when I went to see my sister in 1924, I was not ashamed to show myself in front of her.

My father's flat had three rooms, a living room, a bedroom, and a kitchen. In one corner of the kitchen was a door that led into a lavatory—a sink and toilet; there was no bathtub or shower stall. My father told me how to walk to the bathhouse, three blocks away, where showers were free if you brought your own towels and soap. If you wanted a tub, it cost ten cents. Walking to the bathhouse was no hardship, and when winter came, I liked the walk even more. I loved walking in the snow. The fact that I just came from a hot shower into near zero weather didn't bother me at all. Up to the time I came to the States, I never had a cold. Even in the States I don't believe I had my first cold until I was here a few years.

In 1923 my father bought a car, a four door, black sedan. He paid cash for it, one thousand dollars. Now instead of the family coming to visit us, we went to them. We had breakfast every Sunday morning in a different house. My father's car was the first one in this large family. He was also the first one to have a telephone in his house.

My father was very modern. He wanted to teach me to drive his car even though few women drove then. He took me out to a wide street, put me in the driver's seat, and explained to me how the gears work and where the brake is. I drove a couple of blocks without turning or stopping. Then came my downfall because we came to a stop sign. Long before we came to the sign, my father told me to stop. I stopped about six inches away from the car in front of me. My father said that was enough driving for me, a close miss is as good as a hit.

A few months after I came to the States, I wanted to go to work. I didn't know what I could do or where to look for work. My sister-in-law's sister offered to look in the newspaper to see what jobs were offered, and when she found something she thought I could do, she would take me there and get the job for me. She, herself, was a very busy person with three small children and helping her husband in his grocery store.

She took me to a place where they needed girls to trim hats. She explained to them that I can't speak English but was a good worker. Of course I never did any work except digging potatoes, but she had done that kind of factory work before she was married, and she told me it was simple; I will be able to do it. She was right. My job was to put a ribbon around a hat and add some plastic cherries or flowers. Most of the hats were just a shape made of straw, dyed different colors. I was paid nine dollars a week for my labors.

Actually language wasn't a problem, for the foreman and several of the girls were Jewish. We spoke Yiddish, but everyone was trying to teach me English. In a small way it helped; yet, when I was eighteen and wanted to have my picture taken, I was hard put to make myself clear to the photographer. I still have the picture.

With my father's help, I learned to read a little too. I read an ad for a men's shirt factory on Washington Avenue between Thirteenth and Fourteenth Streets. The ad read that they will teach a person to work on an electric machine, and the pay was twelve dollars a week. More money and, especially, learning to work on a machine was a great inducement. I learned to work on a buttonhole machine and a button machine. The latter required more expertise, and I could ask for higher pay.

Our relatives were always trying to make a match for my father, especially after they found out that my mother was dead. My father said that he didn't want his daughter to come home to a step-mother. He would wait to marry again until after I came to St. Louis. Now I was there three years. I was nineteen. Albert, the younger of my two brothers, had married and moved out of town. There was only myself and my father at home. My relatives saw no reason why my father shouldn't marry now. I had my own plans. I wanted to go to New York and live with my sister. I missed her very much; she was like a mother to me. But after all the years my father had waited to have me with him, I couldn't just leave him all alone. I felt if he got married, it wouldn't matter too much to him if I went away.

A likely prospect was found, and my father went to meet her. After several meetings he brought the woman to our house to meet me, my brother, and sister-in-law. My father's main concern was whether I would get along with her. Not knowing anything about the woman, I praised her to high heaven. In years to come I was glad I did. They lived happily together for nineteen years. It was a great sorrow to my father when she died.

We did get along very well. I used to take her to the movies (my father never went to a movie), and she would boast to her friends and relatives of our relationship. I waited three months after they were married to tell my father that I wanted to visit my sister. He thought it was right I should go, for I hadn't seen Mollie in three years. Of course the understanding was that I would stay a month or so and then come home.

Mollie was expecting her first child. That gave me an excuse to stay a little longer. I got a job in New York and stayed on. Even my step-mother became annoyed by my staying away from them that long. She said people would think we didn't get along.

In the spring I came home, but in the fall I went back to New York. I had my own money. My father couldn't stop me. I set a pattern; every spring I came home, and every fall I went to my sister. This going back and forth lasted five years.

Chapter Eight

Mollie gave birth to a little boy November 4, 1924. She was very glad to have me stay on. Besides her husband, I was the only relative she had. By that time I was able to read all the ads in the newspaper. I was a regular weekly reader of *The Saturday Evening Post*. This magazine published work by the best of the current writers. Will Rogers always had a humorous article making fun of politicians, and I also laughed at the short stories of P.G. Wodehouse and Arthur Train. Now I borrowed books in English from the library, not books in Yiddish.

My very first job in New York was in a dress-making establishment on Madison Avenue. It had a woman's name, but I don't remember it. It was on the second floor. It wasn't a factory, it was more like the dressmaker that my mother had make my sister's and my dresses. But while that dressmaker had only two girls working for her, here there were about half a dozen working.

The ad said it would be a good chance for a young person to learn fine dress-making. I remembered how I loved going to the dress-maker to look at Parisian patterns, to look at bright colored cloth. That was in Brest-Litovsk. Here in New York the cloth would be richer, the dresses nicer. I wanted to be a dress-maker.

Mollie's husband told me it would be easy for me to find the place since we lived between Fifth and Madison. I just needed to go farther downtown. I don't remember whether the place was in the forties, fifties, or sixties. I found it and was hired. Nine dollars a week was the pay; not much, but the chance of sometime becoming a famous dress-maker was what I wanted.

My job was pulling bastings. Everything that was sewn was first basted. The fabric was fine, and one had to be careful not to pull on the fabric too hard. I pulled basting and basting. I thought, one of these days they will run out of basing, and I will be given something to do of real value. I pulled basting for five or six weeks, and I saw that before I am fifty, I will not work on anything else. I left to look for something more lively than pulling threads from silks and satins.

I found a job in a shirt factory putting buttons on men's shirts. I don't remember where it was, but it was a very long ride. One morning, going to work on the dreary subway, I thought, "I wish the factory would burn up." I got off the subway and walked to my place of work. It was a corner building. When I got near, the factory was in flames. The boss and other workers were standing around looking at the fire while the firemen were pouring water on the building. I turned around and went home. I didn't even bother to collect my last week's wages.

I decided it was time for me to go back home. I stayed in St. Louis until fall. My nephew was almost a year old. I wanted very much to see him. When I came back to New York, I again started to look for a job. My only skill was to run a sewing machine. I saw an ad that said, "Plain sewing." I went there and got the job. After working there a couple of weeks, it dawned on me that all the women working there were much older than I. In fact there wasn't one young person, and the sewing I did was always on black cloth. One day I asked the gray-haired woman next to me what we were making. She laughed and looked slyly at me and said, "Shrouds." At the end of the week I collected my pay and never went back.

The job that I worked at the longest was in a hat lining factory. It was just making a seam on one side of the lining. The cloth came in layers, cut on the bias. We kept the layers on our laps.

The sewing machine pushed the fabric through to a box on the other side of the machine.

I didn't know that the layers of lining were counted, and a figure was kept on who made the most seams. The work was monotonous, and I tried to make a game of it. Could I be an automaton? I could. While the machine was sewing a lining, I would guide it through the needle with one hand while picking up a lining with the other hand. Just as the needle made the last stitch, I would have the next piece of work right in place. The other girls would pick up a piece of lining with both hands and give it a shake before sewing it. This was not necessary at all. I was less tired than the girls who shook the cloth. It was extra work to do that, while I sat perfectly relaxed—no bodily motion.

Friday was payday. I was getting fourteen dollars a week, and I got another little envelope. The foreman, a very handsome young man—I, like all the girls, was in love with him—explained to me that the little envelope contained five dollars. I had won the prize that week for making more linings than anyone else.

I won the five dollar prize for several weeks. Then the policy was changed. Instead of money, the girl who sewed the most seams would be given an afternoon off with pay. Maybe they thought that if I was gone for an afternoon, other girls would have a chance to win the prize again, and they would be more interested in speed. Even with taking my afternoon off, I still won. Week after week I had a free afternoon.

Being in New York didn't just mean to me a job and work. I wanted to see the city; I wanted to see how other people lived. I heard that in Long Island lived very rich people. I wanted to see their houses and perhaps see some of the people living there. Going on the subway I had noticed a sign to Long Island. I took that train and got off when we crossed the river. What I saw, I realized I had no way to get to what I wanted to see. I took the next train back.

I wanted to see Chinatown. That wasn't hard. I was told where to get off the subway, and when I get to Mott Street, that's Chinatown. I came to Mott Street. It was a long street with buildings on both sides, all doors closed, no cars on either side, no men, woman, or children. I have never seen a street so quiet. When I was halfway through I got scared; the complete stillness scared me. There wasn't even a dog or a cat around.

I had a girl friend in Brest-Litovsk who was also going to America, and she asked me to look her up when I got there. She was going to a sister in Brooklyn. What did we know where St. Louis is and Brooklyn is? I promised to come see her, and she gave me her sister's address and married name.

Of course when I was in St. Louis, I realized that I will never see my friend. But here I was in New York, and was told that going to Brooklyn is no great deal. I went to Brooklyn, and when I got out of the subway, started asking people where the street was that I am looking for. I found the street, found the number of the building, but when I rang the bell, the woman who answered the ring never heard of my friend's sister. I stood there thinking, "What do I do now. I am so far from the subway, I am lost. How can I find my friend, a stranger in a strange city." I looked about me and saw a grocery store. In those days there were small, individually owned stores every few blocks. I went into the store and asked the man behind the counter if he knew my friend's sister since, if she had ever lived at that address, she must have shopped there. I was lucky. He not only knew her, he knew where she lived now, and he gave me instructions how to get there.

I found the sister, and she was so happy to see me. My friend was at work, but, of course, I had to stay to dinner and even overnight. When we heard somebody coming, she hid me in a closet, and when her sister came in, she said, "Guess who's here?" We had a very happy time. To come from where we were and to be able to meet in America is like being born again.

In my time in New York, Fifth Avenue had two way traffic and the green Fifth Avenue bus going uptown and downtown on the same street. Traffic was much lighter; one didn't have to wait too long before crossing the street. Along the park side of the street were benches.

I don't remember how I met my two girl friends; they were sisters. One was blond, and one had brown hair like my own. They lived with their parents, just the two sisters, and one brother. As long as I lived in New York, nine months out of the year for five years, they were my friends.

By the time I met them, I had already seen the sights a New Yorker would not deign to see. But there were other places they would like to go that they were too timid to go themselves. I seemed to be the brave one. When they mentioned a dance hall to which they would like to go if I would go with them, I jumped at the idea. There was one evening in the week girls went in free, men had to pay a dollar. And to dance with the girls, boys had to buy tickets for ten cents. I think that that particular dance hall still operates. The first time we went there I didn't notice anything strange. We had a lot of partners, and everyone was very nice; no bad language, no smirks. The men would dance with us, and when the music stopped, our partners would thank us and sometimes offer to buy us a coke.

We went there two or three times. The last time we were there I noticed some girls were way overdressed. We just wore simple dresses, but the others wore evening gowns. In the washroom I overheard one girl complaining to another about her partner, the last man she danced with. Listening to their conversation, I realized these girls got paid for dancing with the men. I, and my friends, could refuse to dance with someone who didn't look good to us, but these girls had to dance with everyone. The men gave them tickets that they bought for ten cents; after the dancing was over the girls got paid according to how many men they had danced with. The men who danced with us gave their tickets to a girl who stood at the entrance to the dance floor. I also realized that if we weren't there, the girls would have more tickets and make more money. They deserved every penny they made. We didn't go to the dance hall again.

In the evenings my friends and I would walk up and down Park Avenue. There were benches against the wall of the park; when we got tired, we could sit down. On One Hundred and Thirtieth St. about a block west of Fifth Avenue, was an ice cream parlor. We would go there two, three times a week. I was surprised that there were so many young men having ice cream whenever we came there. My friends explained to me that there was a university not too far away. I guess that's why my friends wanted to eat ice cream so often. The ice cream was good, and the dishes had fantastic names, but it didn't lead to any dating.

My girl friends took me to a play on Broadway on a Saturday afternoon. I didn't know what the play was called, nor did I know who was in it. Perhaps they told me who was in it and what it was called, but I didn't know anything about plays and actors. I don't remember whether it was in the first or second act, a young woman came on stage in just a slip, nothing else, just a slip. I told my friends that I don't want to see any more of the play; I want to go home. Years later I saw Mae West in the movies, and that was the actress, except when I saw her on Broadway, she was much slimmer.

I was in New York in 1927 when Charles Lindbergh came back from his lone flight across the Atlantic. Everyone talked about the great feat he accomplished. There was a big parade on Fifth Avenue. Telephone books were shredded. Confetti was made ready to throw on the hero as the parade came slowly down the avenue. I didn't see the parade. Only the buildings facing Fifth Avenue had a view of the parade. People working in these buildings were allowed to look out the windows for a short time. I worked on Thirty Sixth St. about four buildings west of Fifth Avenue. I couldn't see any of the honor paid Lindbergh, and it was galling. I don't know where Lindbergh lived, but because he named his plane "The Spirit of St. Louis," everyone thought that St. Louis was his home. His glory reflected a little on me because I, too, came from St. Louie—as some New Yorkers pronounced it.

I got a job because of Lindbergh. I got tired of being an automaton. I always looked in the Sunday paper for something more interesting. I saw an ad for a job paying eighteen dollars a week in "clean and light surroundings." I don't remember where the place was, but it must have been not far, for I went there on my lunch hour. It was a small place on the second floor. The windows were nice and clean, the sun shining in. It seemed like a very pleasant place. The man who interviewed me, I recognized as the boss. He asked where I worked before. I didn't want to tell him that I worked just a few blocks away, for then he would know that I am job-jumping. People who do that are not very welcome. By the time they've learned what they are to do, they are already looking for another job. I told the man I came from St. Louis, and he wouldn't know the place where I had worked there. As soon as he heard where I came from, he said I had the job. He said, "Anyone coming from the same city as Lindy, can always work for me!"

What was made in that place was little girls' dresses. The job was easy; I had to make a certain seam; everyone else had different parts to sew, and the little dresses were made. After working there a couple of months, it was time for me to go home for a visit. I promised to come back, but I was a job-jumper.

When I came back to New York, I went back to the hat linings. Some of the young girls there were my friends. We would go to lunch together, and sometimes take off a day to go to Coney Island to go swimming. Another reason I went back there was that the same company had a factory in St. Louis. I just had to say where I had worked in New York, and I was put to work. The pay was only thirteen dollars a week in St. Louis, and there was no prize system.

It wasn't the more money I made in New York that drew me to that city. By that time my sister also had a little girl. Mollie's two children were the magnet that drew me to New York. I loved those children so much, it was an effort to part with them, but part I did, for I fell in love on those visits home.

Chapter Nine

My going to New York in the fall and coming home in the spring lasted for five years. Jake and Minnie, my brother and sister-in-law in St. Louis took me under their wing. They took me with them visiting their friends and on picnics which were very much in style then. Most Sundays we would go to Forest Park on the hill, or as it really was called, to the Pavilion. The Pavilion was a large building that had a stand dispensing soft drinks and ice cream. There were no sides to the building. It was open to the out-of-doors, and under the roof were tables and benches.

It seemed to me that on a Sunday the whole Jewish population of St. Louis was on the hill. My cousin, Lena, gave her younger son's Bar Mitzvah party there on the Sunday after his Bar Mitzvah.[8] It was catered. The truck with the food drove up as close as it could come to the tables. Then the caterer's men brought paper tablecloths, paper plates and napkins. I think it was a very nice party and the whole family could come. Otherwise we would have had to rent a hall. This was much nicer. It was a sad day in Jewish quarters when it rained on a Sunday.

The people my brother knew were just like him, married two or three years with one or two small children. In the park the children could toddle around, play games, and their parents were free to talk, gossip, and play cards. The road where there was traffic was too far away for the children to walk to. No thought was given that a child will be kidnapped or some harm befall it, and no child was ever missing from the hill.

Jake introduced me to a girl about my own age, and she introduced me to some of her friends. Forest Park wasn't the only place where picnics were enjoyed. There was a smaller park, I don't remember the name, where these girls took me. Dorothy was the first girl I met with my brother's help. Another girl was Lily and one was Esther. There were a couple more girls. Though I can recall their faces, I can't remember their names. All these girls had come from Poland or Latvia and weren't in the States much longer than I. Naturally our English wasn't very clear. We talked Yiddish. Though sometimes we would try out our English on one another, most times we spoke Yiddish. It follows that we would only go where other Jewish people went. We went to that smaller park several times; it was more enticing. There was a dance floor and musicians played dance music. And there were young men just off the boat to dance with. It cost 50 cents to get in the part of the park where the dancing was.

On one of our Sunday visits my father took me to a family that was slightly related to my brother's wife. There were three boys and two girls in the family. The younger girl, Sarah, told me that on Wednesdays she goes to watch baseball; it is Ladies Day and costs only a quarter to get in. I didn't know what baseball was, but I thought it would be nice to go out. We made up to meet in front of the baseball park. My father told me what streetcars to take to get there. We met and I very much enjoyed the game. It was similar to the *polante* game the boys played in Brest-Litovsk and wouldn't let me join.

With Sarah Dolgin I went many times to watch the Browns and the Cardinals play ball, but the time Dorothy and I made up to go to the Forest Park Theater, it didn't work out very well. We lived in different parts of town and both of us would first have to go downtown to take the streetcar that would take us to the theater. We were to meet at Seventh and Washington. I got off at Seventh and Olive and walked the few blocks to Washington. I was there first. I waited for some time and it started to rain; there was no place to hide; all the stores were closed on Sunday in those days. There wasn't anything I could do but walk back to Olive and wait for a streetcar back home. I had on a green crepe de chine dress and a straw hat with a wide brim. The dress shrank to above my knees and the hat flopped all over my face. Dorothy told me later she didn't come because it was raining.

When I decided to go to New York I went around saying good-bye to all my friends. A few days before I left, my father told me that one of the Dolgin boys was helping a cousin of his to open up a store just a few blocks from where we lived. My father told me that it would be nice if I went over and said good-bye to Mike. I went there, Mike opened the door for me, but there was another young man standing on a ladder, knocking nails into a wall. Six years later that young man became my husband.

When I came back to St. Louis in the spring, I spent most of the time in my brother's house. Jake had a grocery store and lived above the store. My sister-in-law was so very good to me; she wanted me to stay with them all the time. Of course, I didn't, but I slept there many nights when they took me some place and we came home too late for me to go home.

I would go downstairs to the store and help my brother wait on customers. One day he introduced me to an elderly man whose family had recently come to St. Louis. The elderly man was very jolly. He would talk to me and ask if I had a boyfriend. When I told him I had no boyfriend in St. Louis or New York, he told me he had four sons and that I would be just right for his third son. To this man I looked fourteen years old. Of course it was a joke. I didn't meet any of his sons at that time.

In my third year of coming home each spring and working in my brother's store, a young man came in, a friend of my brother's. Jake introduced me to him and told me that he was that old man's oldest son. He was the man I had seen on the ladder. His name was Joseph Tamarkin. I didn't pay much attention to him; he wasn't my type. He had light brown hair and blue eyes. I went for the dark handsome men. But Jake and Minnie didn't bother about my likes. They started to invite that young man to Sunday breakfast, since on Saturday nights I most often slept over. And Joe started coming to my brother's store more often.

When fall came around I was getting ready to go back to New York. One day my brother told me that Joe had a car accident; I should go to visit him in the hospital. I went. When I got there I found he had two other visitors, his sister, Ruth, and her husband. I didn't stay long. I told him I am leaving for New York in a few days and will see him next year. His sister and her husband insisted on taking me home. I didn't want the favor, but I couldn't get out of it. On the way I realized why she wanted to take me home. She wanted to know how well I knew her brother and am I really going to New York. I told her I had my ticket for the trip bought already.

When I came to New York I missed the young man that didn't come up to my standard of the kind of man I would like. Since I had seen him so many times in my brother's store and had Sunday breakfasts with him and even went to see him in the hospital, it would be nice to write him a few words to wish him a quick recovery from his accident. But as much as my father tried to teach me English, it didn't come up to letter writing, and I was embarrassed to write in Yiddish because Joe told me he was going to night high school. I felt very bad. I did start writing, but I knew it wasn't good. I never did write a letter to him though I had many samples I had tried out in my drawer. I looked at what I had written and felt if I sent him a letter that badly written, he would never want to see me again. And that was at a time that I could read English books and magazines, but writing was beyond my powers.

I am now thinking, when did I learn to write? And now it comes to me that after I was married several years, my husband, your grandfather, wanted me to pay some bills. He gave me the checkbook and told me to write out checks; I could sign my name to them. I learned writing as best I could making out checks. My husband's sister, Ruth, lived in Massachusetts. She sent me china as a wedding present. I remember my anguish that I couldn't write her a thank-you note. Several months passed and Ruth hadn't heard from me. She wrote to her sister, Mona, if Mona knew whether I received the gift. Mona told me to write to Ruth. I did write a note. What I said and if she could read it, I don't know. I suppose it was good enough; she didn't complain.

When I came back to St. Louis in the spring, Jake and Minnie took charge of me again. And now I knew some people of my age. Something must have been done for the young people to be able to meet. The third floor of a building was assigned to them. There was another organization on the second floor; I don't remember what was on the first floor. Dorothy and I used to go there in the evening. There I met more young people. What they were trying to do was to put on a play. I don't remember what it was about, but I had a part. I was a little girl in a blond wig. I had no lines; I was supposed to sit in front of a piano and pretend to play it. We put on the play in some small hall allotted to us. People came to see it and paid money. The money was for future undertakings, but I was no longer a part of that group.

The New York Yiddish newspaper, the *Forward*, gave a ball (that's what it was called) in New York every winter. St. Louis readers decided there's no reason why St. Louis can't do the same. My brother told me that he had tickets to this dance affair. And of course I went wherever Jake took me. When Minnie and I got dressed up to go, to my surprise, Joe showed up. He, too, was going to the same affair. I knew it was all arranged by my brother. I didn't care.

At the party were Dorothy and her girlfriends whom I now knew by name. I don't think I can describe my euphoria at being the only girl there with a date. Joe and I danced awhile and then we went out for a walk. I don't remember what we were talking about; I suppose about books. When he asked me to get *Silas Marner* for him out of the library since I lived so close to a library, I was impressed with his choice of reading matter. I didn't know he needed the book for school. He had to write a paper on it.

A few days later he suggested I come along one evening to his school. He picked me up in his truck. He didn't have a car; a truck was more useful to him. On the way home we had an argument. I can't think what it was about. I told him I didn't want him to talk to me all the way home, just to drop me off at my brother's.

I went back to New York without seeing Joe again. When I came into work I found a new girl was hired while I was away. The girl looked so much like me. She was my height with black, short, curly hair just like mine. I thought it would be fun to have a friend who looked so much like me.

At lunch time I asked her if she would like to go out to lunch with me. When she said she would be glad to have lunch with me, I realized she spoke English as the English do. I liked her accent. We became very good friends. She told me she came from England. The whole family moved to Canada, and then they decided to move to the States. They lived in Brooklyn on 14th St. in a one-family house. They had plenty of room, and I was to come and stay over the weekend.

And that is what I did. I would come on a Saturday, stay until Sunday night, and then her brother would take me home on the subway. It took an hour each way. I felt sorry for the young man to have to travel so much on the subway, but her mother wouldn't hear of me going on the subway alone at night.

One Saturday when I came, my girlfriend told me she was seeing a young man and that he will come and bring a friend of his for my date. It turned out that my date was dark and handsome, just the kind of man I had thought I would one day marry. And he seemed interested in me. I didn't give him a second thought. I was just waiting for the time I will go back home and see the man I argued with. I was only thinking of the man with light brown hair, blue eyes, and fair skin. I didn't go back to New York that fall.

While my girlfriend in Brooklyn was trying to find a man for me, Joe was dating a nice looking blonde. After the third date it came to nothing. Joe was sitting in her house, talking to her parents after bringing her home. Her brother came in waving an umbrella and said to his parents, "Look what I picked up in the restaurant. It's almost new." That was their last date. Joe didn't want to marry a girl from a family where it was alright to steal umbrellas.

The jolly old man whom I met in my brother's store and who wanted me to marry his third son died that year, 1929. Joe came to see me at my brother's store and we spoke to each other as if there never was an argument. We saw each other every day since I was at my brother's most of the time. For Joe it was convenient to come and see me. He and his brother had a grocery store a few blocks away.

Sometimes Minnie would ask Joe to come to Sunday breakfast. One Sunday he saved my life. I was eating toast and drinking coffee. Someone said something funny, I started laughing, and a piece of toast got stuck in my throat. I coughed and choked; I was rolling on the floor and thinking: "This is the end." I can really say that not only in drowning does one's life go through one's mind to the end. It was very much like the time I almost drowned. One sees one's life going in review. Your future grandfather gave me a whack on my back; the toast popped out of my throat.

It was no mystery to both of our families that we see each other every day, spend every free moment together. It was becoming serious and both sides felt they had to give advice. My father said I shouldn't rush into marriage. My father knew Joe; he met him in my brother's store several times. He thought Joe was a nice young man, but he thought I could do better than marry a grocery man. Joe's side of the family thought that he could do better than marrying a girl without money and one so short she may not be able to have children.

Of course we told each other what was being said to us on each side. Joe said he loved me, and he would like to have children, but we will get married and let the future take care of itself.

His sister, Mona, asked him to bring his girlfriend to Thanksgiving dinner. That was very important to me; I wanted to make a good impression. What dresses I had didn't seem to be just right. I went shopping for a "just right" dress, shoes, and bag. In a small store on Washington Avenue I found they carried small sizes. The department stores didn't in those days. I bought a brown silk crepe dress, ankle length, long sleeved, with a high round neck. I felt that neckline would have been nice with some kind of necklace, but I didn't have ánything good. And rather than wear something from the dimestore, it would be better not to wear anything at all.

The skirt of the dress was interesting. It had a panel from right to left and it had a ruffle from waist to hem edging the panel. Since the dress was dark brown, I bought beige hose with a bag and shoes to match to brighten up my very smart dress.

I don't think I went over too well. Mona was a tall blond woman. In my dark dress, with very little make-up, I looked even smaller and skinnier than I was. The next day my fiancé told me that his sister wanted to know why I am wearing such a dark dress. The smartness of my dress made no impression. However, she made no other remark about my person. She didn't agree with her aunts about my size or about the fact that I had no money. I believe that she was as shy to meet me as I was to meet her.

The business didn't do too well. The brothers decided to give up the store and look for jobs. Joe's brother found a job as a butcher in a large grocery store. Joe saw an ad for a salesman in a wholesale importing house. The owner was German, and he imported from Germany, cheese, pickles, sardines, and other delicacies. St. Louis had a large German population. South St. Louis was known as Germantown.

The owner told my fiancé that he never hired a Jew, but he liked his looks and will take a chance on him. Joe did real well. Before long he was the highest paid man; since it was a commission job, the more he sold, the more the salesman got paid. The other salesmen complained that the Jew is making more money than they do. My fiancé never stopped for a short beer. He never went to a weekday afternoon baseball game. He worked from nine in the morning until five in the afternoon.

As the economy became worse, retail business slowed down, but Joe was still making good wages. A week before our marriage he was fired. The owner said he had nothing against him, but he didn't like discord in his house. I am happy to report the old established importing house went bankrupt three or four years later.

My future husband lived with his brothers and sister in a two family flat on Crest Avenue. He lived downstairs; Mona, her husband, and two children lived upstairs. Their sister, Ruth, bought the house for the family when they came to St. Louis. Ruth bought the house with a small down payment. Renting one of the flats would help to pay up the mortgage. When Mona got married, she moved upstairs. The whole family formerly lived in Pittsburgh where Ruth lived at the time.

Crest Avenue was just two or three blocks long, and every house on both sides looked exactly alike. Unless you looked at the number, you could walk into your neighbor's house and think you were home. That's what really happened to Joe before we were married. He used to come home for lunch and his youngest sister, Mary Ann, would prepare his lunch and have it ready when he came home. One day he came into the house and saw no lunch on the table. He yelled out: "Where is my lunch?" The neighbor woman came in from the kitchen and said; "Mr. Tamarkin, I wasn't expecting you for lunch." Rather embarrassed, he apologized, and went into the house where his lunch was ready.

Chapter Ten

We were going to get married. A date was set. Our birthdays were both in June; the 15th of June, Joe's birthday, was just ten days after mine. We decided to get married on his.

I told my father; Joe told his brothers and sisters. I bought a wedding dress. It wasn't white; it wasn't that kind of a wedding. My dress was ankle length. It flared from the waist down. It had a big round collar that covered my shoulders like short sleeves. It had a white background with large blue flowers.

On Saturday I put on the dress and we had our picture taken. On Sunday we were married. My father's and my guests were Jake and Minnie. On my fiancé's side he had his three brothers, Marshall, Bill, and Charles, and his two sisters, Mary Ann and Mona, and Mona's husband, Herman.

We were married in my father's living room. After the ceremony there was cookies and wine. The guests didn't linger long; everyone left except Mona and Herman. They took us on a ride around the city and around the country where the big and beautiful homes were. After a couple of hours we went home. They to their upstairs flat on Crest Avenue, and we to the downstairs flat in the same house. Joe's three brothers and Mary Ann were waiting for us. Mary Ann cooked something, I don't remember what, for dinner, and we sat around and talked. The flat had two bedrooms, a dining room and a living room. We slept in one bedroom, the brothers slept in the other bedroom, and Mary Ann slept in the living room on the sofa.

That was how my wedding day was spent. It was worse the next morning; when I got up I had to make breakfast for six people—in a strange house, in a strange kitchen. Then I realized I didn't marry a man, I married a family.

About a month or two later Mona and Herman decided that their flat is too small for them. They rented a large apartment on Westgate Avènue. My husband put up a sign: Flat For Rent. But no one came to rent it. Then Joe noticed that every other house had such a sign on their windows.

Joe out of a job, the other flat staying empty, he couldn't meet the payments on the mortgage. We lived there for three months, then the bank took over the house, and we had to get out.

Mary Ann and Charles went to stay with Mona. Joe's other brother, Marshall, rented a room somewhere; he was a butcher, he could pay his rent. Bill went East to stay with Ruth. Aunt Fannie, she was married to my husband's uncle, gave us a room in her small one family house. It was very good of her to take us in. The house had only three bedrooms and she had four children. We stayed with Aunt Fannie for three months.

At the time we lived with Aunt Fannie, my husband still had the small truck. We would leave early in the morning, and, if asked why we were in such a hurry to leave, we would say that wherever we had to look for a job, we wanted to be first. It was really so that Aunt Fannie wouldn't have to make breakfast for us, her husband, and four children. And we wanted to be alone.

The truck was our second home. Joe and I would drive to Pratzel's Bakery, buy sweet rolls and a bottle of milk, and we would sit in the truck and have our breakfast. I never enjoyed a breakfast better than having sweet rolls and milk on the front seat of a truck. One day my husband came back with six cinnamon rolls. It was almost the end of a perfect marriage. Joe didn't know, even I didn't know, that I don't like the smell of cinnamon.

He loved it. Peace was brought about when he went back and got two cheese rolls. I don't know about Joe's coffee drinking before marriage, but I seldom drank coffee, and milk for breakfast was always my drink. I know I didn't miss coffee as I would now.

We would go looking for jobs. I went to the factory where I used to work in the summers when I came to visit St. Louis, but there was no more factory; it was closed. Joe worked in a grocery store two days a week, 10 hours a day, for five dollars a day. There was really nowhere to find a job. We would drive around and around. Noon we would stop at my brother's store. Jake and Minnie were always happy to see us. We would spend a few hours there just to pass the time. Late in the afternoon it got busy in the store, and we would leave.

Memory seems to press time together. I remember it was getting dark and we were hungry. Dear Lizzie, now came the meal that was best of all. Your grandfather would get Jewish rye bread, half-sour pickles, sliced salami, and Coca-Cola. Never did anything taste so good. We were together, alone, and very happy. It was like a joke: we knew that some day we will eat better, but nothing will taste as good, because the world was still before us.

We didn't always have it so good. We were invited to dinner by my father and my brother. Mona and Herman would have us over for dinner, and then take us to a movie. Most times Mona and Herman would take us along when they went to visit Herman's father and mother.

Of course we were still looking for jobs. Even Herman's father was trying to get a job for my husband. He had many friends who in their businesses hired men, but they said they weren't doing any hiring. They were firing the latest men hired.

Herman's father was a builder. He had built and sold many properties. He had built a large building on Grand Avenue. The upper stories were apartments, the ground floor was stores. None of the stores nor the apartments were rented; 1930 was a bad year for real estate. He said he would give us a store, rent free, until we could pay the rent. He said all his friends will flock to a sandwich shop, especially if we make good coffee.

There was a shop that sold restaurant equipment. The name, I believe, was Benzinder. My husband went to that shop. When a salesman asked what he can do for him, he said he wants to talk to Mr. Benzinder. The salesman took my husband to Benzinder's office. Joe explained to Mr. Benzinder that he has no money and Mr. Mayer, the builder, is giving a store free of rent until he can show a profit. What my husband wanted Benzinder to do is equip the store with all things needful for a restaurant: an ice cream counter, tables and chairs, and all that is needed in the kitchen—cooking pots, frying pans, an ice box, and cutlery for the tables, and, of course, dishes to serve the food in. Oh yes, a large coffee-pot and a register. The things would come to several thousand dollars. My husband told him he hasn't got a penny. Mr. Benzinder wasn't a young man; he had been in that business for many years. Such a crazy deal had never come his way. He looked at Joe for a while; then he said: "I'll do it."

Benzinder was as good as his word. It wasn't a very large store, but it was big enough for a counter running on the left side as one entered from just a few feet from the door to almost the full length of the store. The counter was white plastic laminate. Sunk into it were several metal containers for ice cream. I don't remember how many flavors were then in style. We had a machine that made malteds and several ice cream scoops. That was all on the left. On the right we had square tables that sat four and wooden chairs to match. I am not going into everything Benzinder gave us, but it was a fully equipped restaurant.

Your grandfather stood by the register to collect the money. In the morning I fried eggs, made toast, fried bacon, and served the customers. With the coffee pot came instructions, how much water to how much coffee. Everybody liked our coffee.

When breakfast was over, I washed the dishes, cleaned the tables, and started a roast for lunch. Sometimes people would want a salami sandwich. Joe would make the sandwich and go back to the register.

We did good business. The place was full in the morning and full for lunch. We would get to the restaurant about six in the morning and closed at seven in the evening. We didn't have any customers for dinner, but young people would come in for ice cream. It was a good place for a sandwich shop; our only competitor was a large, expensive restaurant, the Bevo Mill.

Had we hired a cook and waitress, we would still be in the business. We couldn't do everything ourselves; it made the service too slow. Joe and I knew nothing about how to run a restaurant. At first we did good business, but after a while less and less people came to the place. In three months we had to close the doors; we had taken in only three dollars the whole day. I was so tired, I was glad not to be there in the morning, making coffee, frying eggs, and burning toast.

The five years when I was part in New York and part in St. Louis I managed to save five hundred dollars. Joe wouldn't let me take the money out of the bank. That money was for the time that things will get real bad. That time was now. Joe knew he could sell if he had what to sell. He went to the Swift Packing Co. and made a deal with them that they should pack their mayonnaise under the label "Sunrise." It was common practice for large companies to pack for smaller ones under a different label. Then my husband went to the St. Louis pickle company to pack pickles under his label. And he went to a macaroni company to get noodles to pack under his label.

That's where the five hundred dollars came in. He had no credit rating, and everything had to be paid for on delivery. He rented a very small store; somehow he got a wooden table and chair. I had to sit there the whole day packing noodles into cellophane bags—the most boring thing I ever did. I was pregnant and it was hard to sit still there the whole day. Sometimes we would both work in the evenings. He sold the products under his label and did real well. We no longer lived with Aunt Fannie; we were in business and could pay rent for an apartment.

Then tragedy came. My baby was supposed to be born around the 14th of May. On a Saturday we went to see a movie at the Fox on Grand Avenue. It must have been a very popular movie; I don't remember what it was. As we were leaving the theater there was a lot of pushing and shoving. Everybody wanted to get out first. Somebody gave me a push in my middle. I felt the baby give a turn. After that I didn't feel it again. Monday I went to the doctor. He examined me and told me my baby is dead. He also told me that the same thing happened to the daughter of a doctor friend of his, and they both decided to let the woman carry the baby until its due date. The young woman had a long time to carry the dead baby, she was only in her seventh month, while I should be having the baby soon. This news I had to tell my husband who was in the waiting room.

I began labor the 14th. It was in the evening. Herman, Mona, and Joe drove me to the hospital. The nurses examined me and said it will be a long time before the baby will be born; my relatives could go home. They went. There wasn't anything they could do for me.

The pain increased almost beyond endurance. I wanted to die, the quicker the better. I was looking at the windows to see if I could get to them and throw myself out of the fifth floor. Finally they called my doctor. When he came into the room and took a look at me, he dropped his coat on the floor and started giving orders.

The baby had to be taken with instruments. It was a big boy weighing ten pounds. I wanted to see my baby I will never have, but they said I couldn't see him. But my husband saw him. Joe told me the baby had blond hair and he looked like a six month old baby, sleeping.

I don't know just what had happened when they had to take my baby with instruments, but I was very sick after the birth of my baby. I was in the hospital for six weeks. Even after that I was taken home in a wheel chair; I couldn't walk.

While in the hospital I had great pain in my left hip. Maybe during delivery it was dislocated or fractured. The pain was so great, I wouldn't let the nurses give me a bath or change the sheets on my bed. The doctor prescribed cocaine to still my pain. That helped. After two weeks I was able to sit on my bed and hang my feet down. The next try was to put me in an easy, soft chair for an hour. The doctor came in. He saw me sitting and said: "If the hospital was on fire, you would be the first one out." I tried to make a movement. I looked at him and said: "If the hospital was on fire, I would burn." He believed me. He saw I was helpless. He told me that as much as possible I should try to walk even if I have to hold on to things. I did that. In a couple of weeks I was able to walk; that is, on one foot. To move my left foot I had to bend down almost to the ground.

One day after I left the hospital my husband took me to visit Jake in his store. I was sitting down. A friend of my brother's came in, we were introduced, and then my husband and I went home. The friend saw me walk and remarked to Jake; "I didn't know your sister is a cripple." I mention this because it took months before I could walk without a limp.

Joe ran his pickle, noodle, and mayonnaise business the best way he could while I was unable to help him. He would pack the noodles sometimes half the night and be up in the morning on his truck calling on grocery stores. After a couple of months, walking became less painful for me, and I could sit up for several hours packing noodles.

I became pregnant. We very much wanted to have a baby. I continued with the work. Joe would take me to our little packing place in the morning and pick me up when he was through with his sales. There was no phone in the place where I sat the whole day. Joe couldn't call me. We made up that at certain times I should walk over to the drugstore and call my brother. My husband would call Jake to find out how I am.

One morning my husband took me to my place of work and left to do his. He wasn't gone ten minutes when I began to have labor pains. My baby wasn't due for another two months. Here I was without a phone and didn't know how to reach my husband. I had no money to call a cab. I went to the drugstore and called my brother and told him to try to call stores where my husband sells his wares, perhaps he can catch him. I went back to my place of work and laid down on the floor to wait for Joe to come and take me to the hospital. I was in great fear that my baby will be born before my husband is found. In that case I would have another dead baby.

My brother found my husband in about two hours. I was taken to the hospital. When I came to the hospital, my doctor was there waiting for me. Joe had the foresight to call the doctor as soon as my brother told him I was in labor.

I gave birth to a premature baby boy after carrying him only seven months. The doctor assured me that he was a fine healthy baby weighing five pounds. This time I had no trouble and was able to go home with my baby, your Uncle Allan, after the regulation two weeks.

The real estate business still wasn't booming in 1932. Mr. Mayer hadn't sold even one of the block of bungalows he had built. He told us that we could have a bungalow free of rent until he sells some of them. This was a great boon for us. We had a new two bedroom house, with a living room, dining room, and beautiful bathroom. And that came just in time for now I couldn't help my husband at all. I had a baby to take care of.

Without having to pay rent, things were a little easier. As meager as my husband's earnings were, we were better off than most people. We lived in a nice new house with everything very modern for those times. Herman and Mona, though they lived in a bigger house, didn't have it as good. They lived on what Herman's father gave them. Sometimes Mona would call and ask if they could come over for dinner. I don't believe it was because they didn't have anything to eat. It was just to break the monotony.

After dinner they would take us to a movie. Herman always paid for us. The movie houses were only ten cents per person, but Herman wanted us to go four, five times a week. That counted out for us as real money. On our own we would perhaps go once a week. We were in luck about a baby-sitter. My husband's brother, Bill, came back from living with Ruth, got a job in a delicatessen, and lived with us. He didn't mind baby-sitting for by then my son slept the night through. Of course, if Bill had a date, we couldn't go out.

The other entertainment besides movies that there was, was radio. But one had to have the money to buy one. In my brother's store, as in many other grocery stores, there was a punch card. You could buy a chance to punch out a number for ten cents and sometimes win a prize. Joe punched out one of the last punches on the board and won a radio that was standing right by the board. There was a young black man that tried to win the radio but saw my husband win it. He asked my husband if he would sell the radio to him. Joe would have liked to keep the radio, but we needed the money more. They agreed on a price, but, of course, the young man didn't have the money. He was to pay three dollars a week till it was paid up. The price was thirty-five dollars, but when the man paid up thirty dollars and Joe saw how hard it was for him to keep on paying, he told him to forget the last five dollars.

We lived in the nice bungalow that Herman's father let us live in for more than a year. Then I think he sold the whole row of bungalows to a real estate man. It must have been at a loss, for he was making plans to move to Cincinnati. He bought a distillery and all his children moved with him. We lost Herman and Mona and the free movies.

Chapter Eleven

In 1936 when our son was four years old and our little girl, Pamela, your mother, was a year old, we moved to a two-family house in south St. Louis. Every house on the street was a two-family like ours. Our landlord, a widower, lived upstairs; we lived downstairs. Shaw's Garden, a botanical park, was at the end of the street. There was no through traffic. The children played on the sidewalks, but even if they ran after a ball into the street, there wasn't much danger.

It was a hard-working street. The husbands went to work and the wives stayed home, cooking, cleaning, and taking care of the children. On Saturday mornings, the men took their wives shopping. On Saturday afternoons the women would wash their porches and front steps. Sometimes they would interrupt their work to visit and talk with a neighbor. The men spent the afternoon washing and polishing their cars. It was a one car family street. I called it "The Saturday Street." It seemed to me that the sun always shone on that street. It was peaceful and right with the neighbors talking to one another, giving and asking advice. When we moved away, I always looked for another "Saturday Street." I never saw another street like that.

My second son, your Uncle Maurry, was born while we lived there. When he was about four months old, he used to cry every afternoon around five o'clock. He would only quiet down if he was pushed in the buggy. I would put him in the buggy on the porch, run out every few minutes to give him a few pushes, and then run back in the house to see how the dinner I was cooking was getting along. One day my next door neighbor's husband knocked on the door. He was a teller in a bank and came home earlier than all the other men. He asked me if I would like him to push the buggy up and down the sidewalk to make the baby happy. He didn't do it just once, but for weeks. I can't forget the sight of a man in a three-piece suit pushing my baby. It was a Saturday street with Saturday neighbors.

My husband worked as a salesman for the Metropolitan Insurance Company selling life insurance on commission. It was hard work because his customers were not rich people who could afford to pay their premiums by check once a year or even once a month. Joe had to call on his customers once a week to collect a quarter from this one, fifty cents from that one. Sometimes the poor people didn't have even a quarter to give him, and he would have to go several times to some families. It was discouraging for him to climb three flights of stairs to an apartment to collect a quarter, and often, in those hard years, to come away with nothing. But he kept going again and again. For one thing, he believed in the life insurance he sold. His customers had no savings. If anything happened to the breadwinner, they would have no income and nothing to fall back on. For another thing he was determined to give his children a better life than we had. Many times in the years he worked for Metropolitan he won a prize for being their best salesman.

Not long after Maurry was born in 1938, we moved away from the Saturday street. Our living quarters were becoming too crowded with a third child, and also Joe was always thinking of ways to better our condition. His plan was that we should find a place that would have enough room for our family behind a little store. I could mind the store and the children and help the family's earnings. He found such a place on Plymouth and Ferguson. Besides having a little delicatessen and enough rooms for us, it was on a double lot where the children could play without too much care.

We moved there and were happy there. I did business even though there was a bigger market just across the street. I opened my store at seven in the morning and stayed open until nine at night. The bigger store opened at nine in the morning and closed at six. I was open seven days a week. The bigger store was closed on Sundays. I showed a profit, but after a year and a half, we had to sell the little store and move to an apartment. I was worn out.

While we were living in that apartment your Uncle Stanley was born in 1942. By the time my second daughter, your Aunt Sasha, was born in 1944, we were living in our own single-family house. Even though five is an odd number, to me it seemed three sons and two daughters adds up to a round and sufficient number.

When I started this story I was sixty-nine years old. Now that I am finishing it, I am eighty-five. I won't tell of our children's growing years; the story is not much different from many American families'. The children grew and we prospered. All of our five children graduated from college, two of them got Ph.D's. My husband died when he was only fifty-four. We had celebrated our thirtieth wedding anniversary just a few months before. I wanted to die then too, but I went on living in spite of my wishes. Now thirty years later, I have been a widow for as long as I was married. My sister, Mollie, died two years after Joe did. I left St. Louis thirteen years ago to live in New Haven near four of my children (my youngest child, Sasha, lives in Israel). I have fourteen grandchildren and two great-grandchildren.

One day during those terrible years, a woman digging potatoes next to me turned to me and said in a severe way, "You're the youngest one; you'll live the longest. Remember our suffering and tell of it. Don't let it be forgotten." Dear Lizzie, this story is for you and for her.

Notes

[1] Purim is a joyous Jewish holiday celebrating Queen Esther's bravery in saving the Jewish people from the king's wicked advisor, Haman.

[2] Good holiday, in Yiddish.

[3] Passover is a Jewish holiday celebrating the Jews' freedom from slavery in Egypt. Matzah is eaten, because, unlike bread, it has no leavening in it; according to tradition, the People of Israel were in such a hurry to leave Egypt, they did not wait for their bread to rise. They put it on their backs and let the sun bake it into hard, flat bread.

[4] The rite of shiva is part of the Jewish laws of mourning. The shiva period begins immediately after the burial and lasts seven days. While observing shiva, the mourners sit on low stools as a sign of mourning, usually in the home of the deceased. It is customary for the entire family to sit shiva together. Friends of the family visit each day to recite the Kaddish (mourners' prayer).

[5] On Yom Kippur, the Day of Atonement, Jewish people fast for the day as part of the ritual of repentence and forgiveness.

[6] Emigrants were examined for a host of medical ailments, including trachoma, and some were made to undergo operations or remain behind. See Irving Howe, *World of Our Fathers: The Journey of the East European Jews to America and the Life They Found and Made* (New York, 1976), 39-46.

[7] For many immigrants, the prospect of inspection and possible exclusion from America was overwhelming. Immigration officials checked for contagious diseases, and, after 1917, the government imposed literacy tests as a further means of restricting immigration. Immigration declined during World War I, but with the war's end thousands of refugees fled to America. In a nativist backlash against immigration, legislation in 1921 and then passage of the National Origins Quota Act in 1924 dramatically restricted annual legal entry from Europe, gave decided preference to those from northern Europe, and reduced immigration from central and southern Europe to a trickle.

[8] When a boy reaches thirteen, and a girl reaches twelve, he/she becomes a Bar or Bat Mitzvah, an adult in the eyes of Jewish law. They are now responsible for fulfilling the range of Jewish commandments. The core of the ceremony is reading from the Torah, the first five books of the Hebrew Bible. Many families plan a Bar or Bat Mitzvah party after the ceremony to mark this important rite of passage.

Printed in the United States
769000002B

9 780738 839134